Through
Their Eyes

NEWSWORK 6

Through Their Eyes

Foreign Correspondents in the United States

STEPHEN HESS

BROOKINGS INSTITUTION PRESS
Washington, D.C.

Copyright © 2005
THE BROOKINGS INSTITUTION
1775 Massachusetts Avenue, N.W., Washington, D.C. 20036
www.brookings.edu

Library of Congress Cataloging-in-Publication data

Hess, Stephen.
  Through their eyes : foreign correspondents in the United States / Stephen Hess.
     p.   cm.
  Summary: "Drawing on personal interviews and original survey research, reveals the mindset of foreign correspondents posted in the United States from a wide range of countries, and examines how foreign reporting has changed over the past 20 years."—Provided by publisher.
  Includes bibliographical references and index.
  ISBN-13: 978-0-8157-3584-7 (cloth : alk. paper)
  ISBN-10: 0-8157-3584-7 (cloth : alk. paper)
  ISBN-13: 978-0-8157-3585-4 (pbk. : alk. paper)
  ISBN-10: 0-8157-3585-5 (pbk. : alk. paper)
  1. Foreign news. 2. Foreign correspondents—Interviews. I. Title.
  PN4784.F6H476 2006
  070.4′332097309048—dc22   2005027331

                      9 8 7 6 5 4 3 2 1
The paper used in this publication meets minimum requirements of the American National Standard for Information Sciences–Permanence of Paper for Printed Library Materials: ANSI Z39.48-1992.

Typeset in Giovanni

Composition and design by Circle Graphics
Columbia, Maryland

Printed by R. R. Donnelley
Harrisonburg, Virginia

For

Tobie
mystical at five

May the world always seem
as wondrous to you
as it does today.

Contents

Foreword

Steve Hess's work on the interaction between the press and the government is a signature Brookings product. As a former reporter myself and a long-time admirer of Steve's work, I'm proud to be associated with this, the sixth volume in the Newswork series, which began in 1981 with the publication of *The Washington Reporters*. My predecessor Bruce MacLaury began his foreword to that volume with these words:

"In the vast literature about how Americans govern themselves, the role of the press is often neglected. Yet the press—no less than the presidency, the judiciary, and the legislature—is a public policy institution and deserves a place in explanations of the governmental process."

It's hard to imagine that statement being made today, given what a cottage industry press watching has become, including in think tanks like this one. Yet Bruce was accurately reflecting the degree to which the media were then at the margins of social science scholarship.

Indeed, Steve first had to invent new research tools to understand the press. Realizing, for instance, that many reporters are ill at ease with abstractions, he surveyed them by devising a daily log or diary that required precise information on each story: Events attended? Documents used? Types of people interviewed? On or off the record? In this way he showed how information, even of a presidential cast, is often channeled through Capitol Hill before it reaches the public.

When studying Congress in two of his books, he took such unorthodox approaches as charting every TV camera at Senate hearings for a year, thereby illustrating the media's priorities; exploring the politics of the Congressional Press Galleries; comparing the salaries of press secretaries to those of other staffers and then comparing their place in their office hierarchy to what they said their place was. When interviewing senators, he asked, "The press will put an adjective in front of your name; if you had your druthers, what adjective would you choose?" ("Hard-working" was their favorite.) He then counted adjectives in the leading newspapers. In one study, entitled "I Am on TV, Therefore I Am," he added up how often House members appeared on the television news in their district and discovered, despite what they thought, that it was not very often. One of the joys of reading Steve is that he knows how to be serious without being dull.

For a book on government press offices he spent a year inside the White House, the State Department, the Department of Transportation, and the Food and Drug Administration, watching press officers fight their bureaucracies for the information that reporters want but mostly watching them shout good news and whisper bad news. Peripatetic in pursuing his research, he was at the side of the secretary of transportation within minutes when an Air Florida jet crashed into the 14th Street Bridge in Washington, and he later used that experience in a fascinating case study of how government information officers respond during a crisis.

To gather material for a book examining the U.S. media's coverage of international news, he trailed correspondents in such places as Tokyo, Beijing, Vienna, and Prague, contrasting his observations with content analysis. In this book, that book's mirror image, he looks at other countries' coverage of the United States at a time when what the world thinks of the U.S. government and Americans is of considerable importance to Americans and the government. Some of his conclusions will be controversial, in part because there is no other major research on the subject to test his findings.

Nearly thirty years after Steve began his work, the field of media studies has become not just an accepted part of what public policy research institutions do, but one that policymakers and our other constituencies clearly value. Steve deserves considerable credit for bringing about that change. On May 24, 2004, the Brookings Board of Trustees designated him a Senior Fellow Emeritus. In his case, the well-deserved honor for a distinguished career conveys no hint that he's resting on that or any other of his many laurels. But still to come is a volume, Newswork 7, in which he will return to the beginning of his investigations to sort out what has changed and what has stayed the same in the government/press connection in Washington. The answer, of course, is "a lot," and there's no one who understands both the change and the continuity better than Steve.

STROBE TALBOTT
President, Brookings Institution

Washington, D.C.
November 2005

Guide

The nature of this study and where it fits in the Newswork series

In 1977, shortly after Jimmy Carter became president, I made a wish list of three books that I wanted to write, a trilogy to be called Newswork. The first volume would be a study of reporters who cover the U.S. government for domestic news organizations and of how they organize themselves to do their work. The second volume would cross the aisle to examine how the government conducts its own press operations. The final volume would focus on foreign correspondents in the United States. I hoped that together these books might begin to define the unique web of relationships that exist between the government and the media, relationships that I felt were of growing importance in understanding public policy. I had never been a journalist or a communications scholar. I was merely curious and could find too few books to sate my curiosity. There were a number of memoirs of the "presidents who have known me" variety written by reporters;[1] an excellent but ancient (1937) sociological study of Washington correspondents;[2] a book about government–press relations based on a modest 1961 survey of thirty-eight public information officers and thirty-five journalists;[3] and a splendid 1963 analysis of the diplomatic beat.[4]

The first of the Newswork series, *The Washington Reporters,* was published in 1981; *The Government/Press Connection: Press Officers and Their Offices* came out in 1984. Yet the proposed third volume kept getting pushed aside. My work expanded in other directions, resulting in two books about media coverage of Congress—*The Ultimate Insiders: U.S. Senators in the National Media* (1986) and *Live from Capitol Hill!* (1991)—and another about how the American

1

media cover the rest of the world, *International News and Foreign Correspondents* (1996).

Part of the reason why the subject of foreign correspondents in the United States got preempted by others has to do with the design of operations at Brookings, which I have been content to call my home for more than three decades. While university-based scholars can choose what they want to write about, they must find the time and other resources necessary to do the writing. Brookings scholars, on the other hand, must seek approval of a proposed project from the institution's trustees, and if approval is forthcoming, they are given the time and other resources needed to complete it. (This approval process represents the sole involvement of the trustees in a scholar's project.) That trade-off is one that I have gladly made. And for a number of years, my employers seemed to feel that the foreign press corps was not a high priority and that I could be more usefully engaged in exploring questions related to the U.S. presidency, elections, and civility in the public arena.[5]

The irony of my late start in studying foreign correspondents is that this book now appears at a time of renewed national attention to how the world views Americans and the United States and of the U.S. government's concern about how other people's perceptions could affect U.S. policies. The news is not good. The 2005 *Sixteen-Nation Pew Global Attitudes Survey* concluded that "the United States remains broadly disliked in most countries surveyed, and opinion of the American people is not as positive as it once was."[6] Secretary of State Condoleezza Rice repeatedly lamented that "too few in the world" were aware of the various strengths of the country, such as the "generosity of the American people" or "the protections that we provide for freedom of conscience and freedom of speech," when she announced the appointment of Karen Hughes, one of President George W. Bush's most trusted advisers, as head of the government's "public diplomacy" operations.[7] After U.S. forces entered Iraq, the government's effort to tell its story overseas—public diplomacy to some, propaganda to others—expanded greatly, funded by an annual broadcasting budget of more than $600 million. That effort now included television and radio stations operated by the U.S. government—Al Hurra ("The free one," in Arabic) and Radio Sawa ("Together," also in Arabic) and Radio Farda, in Farsi—and *Hi*, a magazine aimed at Arab youth in their teens and twenties.[8] The State Department even created a web page, "Identifying Misinformation," to respond to conspiracy theories and other allegations.[9]

Surely if foreign correspondents in Washington and New York "significantly influence what foreign audiences in Europe, Asia and elsewhere know and think about the United States," as some scholars note,[10] then a study of who they are, how they work, and what they produce should help explain why the world sees the United States as it does.

The major measuring tool of this study is an extensive questionnaire sent in 1999 to nearly 2,000 men and women whose names are listed in the press gallery section of the *Congressional Directory*, the State Department's *Directory of Foreign Correspondents in the United States*, *Editor and Publisher International Year Book*, *Hudson's Washington News Media Contacts Directory*, *News Media Yellow Book*, and the membership directories of the Foreign Press Association of New York, the UN Correspondents Association, and the Hollywood Foreign Press Association. In short, my assistants and I sought out anyone in the United States who desired to be known as a foreign correspondent. The low rate of return—we received 439 usable responses to the survey—reflects both the subjects' generally high rate of mobility and a number of questionable claims to being a "foreign correspondent," which some individuals apparently think of as a prestigious title that one awards to one's self. Nevertheless, the number of respondents is still three to four times larger than that of any previous study and, for the first time, large enough to examine some correspondents by country. The survey was supplemented by 146 interviews, many transcribed.[11] We asked essentially three questions: *Who* are the correspondents? *How* do they work? *What* do they report? Each of these questions is addressed in a separate section.

First, however, there are two introductory matters that must be attended to. One, correspondents do not work in a vacuum; they must be placed in context. Two, what was the state of foreign correspondents in the United States before this investigation?

Context
What may or may not appear in the world media

Correspondents may come from countries where the practice of journalism differs from the so-called "objective" model; where employers' political or ideological positions shade reporting; where various consumer and commercial considerations must be heeded; where the government owns or controls the media; and where special circumstances exist related to the national literacy rate, level of technology, and even geography. And then, of course, correspondents must take into account any and all overriding national interests. If, as in this study, the country being reported on is the United States, then one of a story's starting points may be anti-Americanism, a sentiment that predates the Constitution.

Then
What we know about foreign correspondents in America, 1955–88

A sizable, permanent foreign press corps took shape in the United States as reporters arrived in 1946 to cover the newly founded United Nations. Based largely in New York and predominantly from Western Europe, these journalists favored analytical pieces that could survive slow transmission by mail. The high cost of sending cables and making telephone calls limited their contact with their editors. They lived by what became known as Barber's axiom, formulated by Stephen Barber, a *Daily Telegraph* (United Kingdom) correspondent: "Happiness is in direct proportion to one's distance from the home office."

The section *Who They Are* includes four chapters that suggest how much "typical" foreign correspondents in America have changed since the days when some had a "special relationship" with the secretary of state.

Patterns
Some findings, 1999–2003

The robust growth in the press corps during the last thirty years or so of the twentieth century was a result in part of TV's coming of age and in part of the arrival of correspondents from Asia, especially from Japan. It was accompanied by a shift in the focus of attention from New York to Washington, reflecting the world's increased interest in the United States as a political power. An unexpected trend also appeared, toward replacing the "classical" foreign correspondent, who circles the world in three- to four-year tours, with journalists who come directly from and return directly to the home office. The latter increasingly are complemented by "foreign correspondents who never leave home": American citizens or others who are hired locally or who are full-time freelancers.

Irregulars
The other foreign correspondents

Our survey turned up a substantial number of respondents—one in five—who considered themselves foreign correspondents although they were not full-time journalists. This group usually flies under the scholar's radar. Many are permanent U.S. residents from other countries. A New York bookseller, for example, wrote about opera for a Hungarian magazine; a Staten Island teacher covered art exhibitions for a Portuguese magazine. Even if their reach is modest in that they are less likely to write for the mainstream media, their output is considerable. Because they often choose to write on cultural topics, their work enriches the scope and diversity of what is reported from America.

Hollywood
A subject the world loves

In 1943 a group of writers banded together to form the Hollywood Foreign Press Association, and by creating a generously distributed award called the Golden Globe, they now play a significant role in film marketing. Often scorned by establishment journalists, they write mostly exuberant celebrity profiles—"Nicole Kidman Is the Epitome of Class," for example, for a Singapore magazine—and interviews that follow a simple question-and-answer format. Their output has expanded with the increased economic importance of movie exports.

In America
It's not like being in any other country

Some correspondents' first impressions of America derive from their earlier experiences as students in the United States, but the first impressions of most come from what they have seen in the movies and television. Notes the distinguished British scholar Jeremy Tunstall, "The media are american."[12] The correspondents find New York, Washington, and Los Angeles cosmopolitan and comfortable places in which to live. Very few of them live outside of those three areas, but today's cheaper air fares and lighter television equipment allow them to cover a vast country, even its small towns, better than previous generations of foreign correspondents could. For some, the process of Americanization—the longer they are in the country, the more "pro-American" they see themselves—may create conflicts with their nation's stereotypes of the United States. Their editors may worry that they are "going native."

The *How They Work* section, consisting of five chapters, begins by making an important distinction between foreign correspondents and most other journalists. The time zone in which foreign correspondents work is almost always many hours ahead of or behind the zone where their home office is located.

Time
Adjusting to deadlines around the world

In this chapter, European and Asian correspondents illustrate the difficulties involved in working ahead of or behind the home office by telling how the time warp affects a typical day. The result is almost always that they work more hours, under more stress, than their domestic counterparts.

Contact
Whereby the home office gains on correspondents

E-mail and cheaper telephone rates now allow editors and producers to stay in constant contact with their correspondents. The Internet and cable TV send headquarters instantaneous and continuous news reports from the United States, and bosses in Europe can now read the *New York Times* before their correspondents in New York City wake up. But the news priorities of foreign desk editors watching CNN may not be the same as those of their correspondents in Washington. Who will be the ultimate judge of what is important—or what is true? There are some variations in the tug-of-war between headquarters and field. Bureaus from small countries continue to maintain considerable independence, as do some highly esteemed correspondents from larger countries. At the major news organizations, however, the distance from the home office is growing shorter and reporters' independence is shrinking.

Access
Who sees whom, when, and why

Foreign correspondents' access to U.S. government officials is based on a sliding scale. Pity the correspondent from a small country of no strategic importance. Niche access may be granted to some, such as Mexican reporters, whose country has produced a sufficient number of American voters. Although lack of access is the press corps's primary complaint, it is a serious problem only when correspondents are trying to reach the highest levels of government.

Help
Foreign correspondents as clients of the U.S. government

The Foreign Press Centers are a small unit of the State Department whose offices in Washington, New York, and Los Angeles once were a sort of social club where correspondents gathered to obtain services that they can now get through C-SPAN, CNN, and the Internet. But its special briefings, tours, and logistical assistance received good grades from our respondents, and such services are an inexpensive component of public diplomacy.

Borrowed News and the Internet
Where correspondents turn for information

Foreign journalists can be no better than the local media, or so it's been said. Some complain that in the United States that suggests too-heavy reliance on the liberal-leaning *New York Times* and *Washington Post*. The Internet, however, with its speed and broad availability, presents remarkable new research opportunities—and the added problem of verifying information. Most troubling, perhaps, is that increasingly correspondents are tied to their computers and the ubiquitous cable news channels and therefore have less time and fewer incentives to leave their office to fraternize with the natives.

The *What They Report* section presents a difficult methodological problem. The world's media consist of thousands of outlets publishing in scores of languages. How does one dam such a vast stream of data in order to measure output and content from America?

One Day
The stories and the categories that they fit in

This chapter presents our solution to the measurement problem, which was to ask correspondents to give us their most recent story and answer questions about how they wrote it. Where did the idea come from? What events were attended, interviews conducted, or documents used to write it? Was the home office involved? Was its involvement typical?

The objective was to create a file of one day's reports from the United States. The material was then sorted into various categories, such as Government: International (foreign policy, diplomacy, military affairs), Dangers (guns, drugs, crime, accidents), and Culture (movies, theater, sports, art, books, society). For one set of correspondents—those from Mexico, Canada, Taiwan, South Korea, and Israel and the surrounding Arab countries—the primary mission was to take the pulse of relations between their country and the United States. Another set, usually from small countries like Finland, sought stories with a "home angle"—in the case of Finland, a reunion of Thomas Jefferson's descendants, some of whom are of Finnish descent. The major western European media had the least interest in folksy news. The Japanese press featured well-researched economic stories. Stories on science and technology were idiosyncratic—some serious, some frivolous, with no discernable pattern. There were cultural stories on everything from vacationing in Key West to the comeback of a Japanese baseball player, although our sample overrepresents this category. In the largest category, stories of breaking international news, there was little evidence that correspondents did much digging for anything other than news that they could borrow.

Now
What we know about foreign correspondents, the present

This chapter reviews the changes that have occurred since our story began. Over the half-century from 1955 to the present, the foreign press corps has become bigger and less print oriented. The percentages of whites, males, and Europeans have declined, as has the practice of "salon journalism" over a glass of brandy and a fine cigar. Because of growth in both government and the domestic press corps, foreigners await access at the back of a longer line. The composition of the foreign press corps differs also in that there are more local hires, free-lancers, irregulars, and those who drop in for short visits ("para-chutists," in the trade) and fewer correspondents who spend their entire careers moving from one foreign assignment to the next. The wonders of technology—the Internet and cable TV—connect them more firmly to their home offices, creating new tensions and at the same time opening new avenues of information.

At least a third of what foreign correspondents report is breaking news—and in Washington, that means what the government is doing. Employers want their own brand on the top stories, a desire that reflects organizational ego more than good editorial judgment. Such stories may resemble doctored translations, which in many cases is what they have to be. Even the greatest foreign operations do not have the time, access, or resources of their U.S. counterparts. But such reporting by translation can be done in other places, releasing the correspondents to do what only they can do, the kind of stories that rely on personal observation.

Our firm impression of foreign correspondents' reportage is that while it can be critical of the United States, it lacks the vituperative edge that characterizes the domestic media's views in many foreign countries, thus offering a balance that otherwise would not be present. At their best, foreign correspondents combine an insider's knowledge of their own country with an outsider's insights into the country that they are assigned to cover. That is a rare opportunity and an important one, especially when the other country has a profound impact on the rest of the world.

With prayer and good luck, there will be a seventh and concluding volume of the Newswork series to bring the enterprise full circle. It will explore the question of what has changed, what has stayed the same, and what the consequences of change or stasis have been since *The Washington Reporters* was published in 1981. This researcher no longer has the time or the eyes and ears to do the job alone. But there is a plan. The Brookings trustees in 2004 honored me with emeritus status and an office (and other services) to continue writing, while the George Washington University honored me with a professorship, a fancy title, and, most important, a group of keen and enthusiastic students to act as surrogate eyes and ears, so that together we can propose some answers for others to question in the future.

Context

What may or may not appear in the world's media

Anthony Shadid, the *Washington Post* reporter who won a Pulitzer Prize in 2004 for his human interest stories from Baghdad, said, in defining foreign correspondence: "It's the freedom to go to a foreign place, try to understand the situation, and tell the story with a critical, sympathetic eye."[1] Between his fine definition and reality exists a variety of obstacles relating to a world of press systems, styles, and standards that often are very different from those in the United States.

This chapter reviews the context within which foreign correspondents in the United States do their work. There is a vast literature on how journalism differs around the world, detailed by country and continent, by type of government, by economic system, by culture and tradition.[2] Scholars note, for instance, the influence in some Asian media of Confucian philosophy, which stresses consensus and cooperation.[3] Others sort media types by "quality, class, prestige."[4] In any case, one must remember that journalists produce a product or a service for an organization and are expected to conform to its expectations.

During the fall semesters in 2001 and 2002, Anne Nelson taught a course at Columbia University's graduate school of journalism called "The U.S. as a Foreign Country." Altogether there were fifty-nine students from thirty-two countries in her classes, and most had been journalists in their home country. They were assigned to monitor two or three news organizations in their own country (or a country where they had lived or worked) to assess its media's perspective on the United States. The 2001 period stretched from the September 11 terrorist attacks on the World Trade Center and the

Pentagon through the U.S. military response in Afghanistan; the 2002 period covered the debate leading to the invasion of Iraq. Several years earlier, in the summer of 1998, two interns at Brookings, Afshin Mohamadi and Matt Segal, had visited fifty-eight Asian, African, and Latin American embassies in Washington, asking diplomats about the habits of the media in their country.[5]

From the Columbia students' papers, supplemented by the Brookings interns' reports, we have identified seven external influences on the way that the news from America is reported: government control, management control, "semi-opinionated" reporting, consumer interest, circumstances, anti-Americanism, and national interest. These are "starting points" for understanding the final product. (All those quoted in this chapter, unless otherwise identified, were students at Columbia's graduate school of journalism in 2001 or 2002, reporting on the foreign media.)

Government Control

Governments expand or contract the media's freedom of expression within their borders. The report on the media in China, by a Columbia student who had worked for the *People's Daily,* explained:

> Literally all Chinese media outlets are still supported and controlled by the government. Although some news organizations are financially self-sustained, their editorial independence is hampered by government manipulation. News outlets are under surveillance and guidance of the Publicity Department of the Communist Party of China Central Committee (the party) and the State Council Information Office (the government). . . . Until 2000 the *People's Daily* never allowed a piece of world news to appear on its front page, let alone play it as a top story. . . . The Publicity Department is said to have given guidelines to the news media to downplay the stories about terrorist attacks in the United States.

Added another student, "The media in China [in 2002] is still under strict censorship by the Communist Party and regarded as [a] propaganda tool."

The Columbia students reporting on Egypt and Singapore also mentioned government control: "The Egyptian national TV channels are run by the government. . . . The Egyptian president appoints the editors of the leading newspapers and the country's news agency"; "The media in Singapore are controlled by the state and state-run companies." And, according to the Brookings interns' reports, the deputy chief of mission of the Myanmar (Burma) embassy noted in 1998 that his country's military government intended to keep "peace, law, and order" in the media in order to set the stage for democracy.

Freedom in the World, an annual global survey produced by Freedom House, divided the world in 2003 into eighty-eight "free," fifty-five "partly free," and forty-nine "not free" countries. China, Egypt, and Burma were listed as "not free" and Singapore as "partly free." The rating combined political rights and civil liberties, including an assessment of freedom of expression. The "largest freedom gap" identified by Freedom House was in the Arab world.[6]

Management Control

Media management directs staff to give consumers a product of a predictable political persuasion. In Britain, according to Simon Bishop's report,

> when someone walks up to a newspaper stand and selects a title, they generally know if they select the *Guardian* the choice of stories and their content will be left-leaning. In contrast, the *Daily Telegraph* is right-leaning. The *Independent* sits to the right of the *Guardian,* the *Times* to the left of the *Daily Telegraph.* Just how far these publications "lean" probably depends on individual interpretation, but everyone accepts the general direction.

Illustrating those differences were the *Guardian's* and the *Telegraph's* dueling headlines on October 22, 2001, for the same story: "Taliban: 100 Dead as Hospital Hit" (*Guardian*); "MoD [Ministry of Defense] Denies 100 Dead in Hospital Attack" (*Telegraph*). Similarly, reporting the results of a poll on attitudes toward the war in Iraq on November 22, 2002, the *Guardian* declared, "Poll Shows Voters Split on Iraq," while the *Telegraph* maintained, "Poll Shows Increase in Support for Action."

In France, wrote Aude Lagorce, "Breaking news coverage is always colored by the political inclination of the paper," an editorial bias that Caroline Chaumont called "the tradition of opinion." The Columbia student analysis of the Italian media made the same point regarding coverage in *La Repubblica* and *L'Unita*. The analysis of three Pakistan papers concurred: "News coverage matches editorial policy."

Management's interests, however, may be more than ideological. Ricardo Caballero of Paraguay's embassy explained that all three major television networks in his country endorsed candidates during elections. One network was owned by a cigarette importer, one by a domestic cigarette manufacturer, and one by a cigarette exporter. Each, perhaps unsurprisingly, promoted a different tariff agenda.

"Semi-Opinionated" Reporting

When news organizations publish or broadcast products of a predictable political persuasion, their reporters may write news stories in ways that are "nonobjective" by mainstream American journalism standards.

In Denmark, explains Jasmina Nielsen, news analysis within newspaper articles "is much more abundant . . . than in the American [press]." While there is a "heavy American journalistic focus on 'facts' and 'balance,' " she writes, "many of the [Danish] journalists do not directly quote experts with different points of view, and occasionally some of the articles lack attribution." This form of journalism tends "to be far more relaxed about the need to source quotes."

There is a fine line between the output of columnists, who are expected to express their own views, and a type of hard news journalism that could be called "semi-opinionated," such as that published in what are called *journaux d'opinion* in France. As *London Times* managing editor George Brock has noted, "Objectivity, as it is generally understood by American journalists, is not a core value for the British."[7] The contrast, as formulated by media experts Bill Kovach and Tom Rosenstiel, is between a "journalism of assertion" and a "journalism of verification."[8]

Consumer Interest

What news organizations cover is influenced by the extent of their consumers' interest in a topic. The only countries with sizable press contingents in the United States are Japan, Germany, the United Kingdom, and Korea. Given the size of their populations, Israel, Taiwan, and Canada are well represented. Most remarkable perhaps, is Scandinavia's presence, if its component countries' correspondents are viewed collectively.[9] The growth of the Japanese press corps in the United States reflects the fact that the Japanese, per capita, read more newspapers than any other people in the world. *Yomiuri Shimbun* is the world's only newspaper whose daily circulation exceeds 10 million, and *Sankei*, Japan's fifth-largest newspaper, circulation 2.9 million, sells more papers daily than France's three national papers combined.[10] Israel, described by Caryn Farber as "a news obsessed and media-savvy culture," often treats events in the United States "as [if] they were domestic."

Other countries, even those with a middling interest in the United States, might appreciate more news if they could afford it or were not so preoccupied with their own problems. Mariana Lemann Ferreira Patino explained that "the devaluation of the *real*, the Brazilian currency, made several news companies limit the number of correspondents in the United States." Diego Graglia titled his report for Nelson's journalism class "Argentina, Too Busy in Its Own Chaos to Think of Iraq." There was only one Argentine television reporter in Manhattan on 9/11.

The Columbia student reports indicated that many countries got the vast majority of their U.S. dateline news from wire services, suggesting a lower interest in foreign news and a diet of reportage that is events-driven, with heavy coverage of official government actions: "Because Philippine news media do not have international bureaus, most relied on wire services for news reports"; "The *New Zealand Herald* was almost entirely reliant on wire reports and syndicated copy"; "The coverage of international news in Chilean news organizations is often limited to what international news agencies are reporting."[11]

But regardless of source, readers always are interested in "their own kind," the so-called home angle story, such as human interest pieces on the Australians or Colombians who lost their lives at the World Trade Center or front-page stories in the Norwegian press about Norway's prime minister's visit to the White House.[12]

Circumstances

A country's literacy rate, level of technology, geography, and particular circumstances affect the type and degree of coverage found in its media. Much of the world may have been focused on Iraq in November 2002, "but in Bhutan," wrote Pema Norbu, "the focus of much heated debate has been our own first nationwide election of village leaders." (There is one national newspaper in Bhutan, and it is published once a week.) "The Kenyan press," reported Kodi Barth, "tends to treat American issues with subtle indifference." And in October 2001, an editorial in the *Philippine Daily Inquirer*, the country's largest English-language newspaper, advised its readers:

> Forget about anthrax. Forget about bioterrorism. We are not going to die from those things. The people of Metro Manila are facing much more lethal, much more immediate threats to their lives and well-being. These threats come in the form of garbage that dots almost every other block of the metropolis.[13]

When Brookings interns Segal and Mohamadi toured Washington's embassies, they learned of countries where television viewing was modest, where there were few stations to choose from, and where few consumers could afford a satellite dish, cable installation, or television set. And newspapers are not always an ideal option. "Civil servants read newspapers; people who live in rural areas don't," said the first secretary of Uzbekistan's embassy. The deputy head of mission at Gambia's embassy told them about the dissemination of information by drums, which he called "tabuleh," and the first secretary at Sierra Leone's embassy explained "bush radio," getting the news from travelers and by word of mouth.

When literacy rates are in the 30 to 50 percent range, the medium of choice is radio, which has the added advantage of being cheap. Besides avoiding the pitfall of illiteracy, it overcomes another kind of language barrier. Not all citizens understand the official language of their country: 450 languages are spoken in Nigeria, and many in Senegal speak languages that are heard on radio but do not appear in newspapers. Such media have little interest in the U.S. or international news.

Anti-Americanism

"Why Do People Hate America?" the *Philippine Star* inquired.[14] "Why Is America Hated?" asked the *Hindustan Times*, posing the question somewhat differently.[15] Perhaps more sympathetic was *Le Monde*'s simple headline: "The Unloved America."[16] What other nation inspires headlines like these?

While some such sentiments relate to the foreign policy of George W. Bush, a vigorous anti-Americanism predates his presidency. And America bashing is not limited to questions of political concern; U.S. popular culture is a popular target. Indeed, political scientist James W. Ceaser locates "a kind of prehistory of anti-Americanism" that existed before the founding of the United States and was noted by Alexander Hamilton in *The Federalist Papers*.[17] "By the end of the nineteenth century," writes Simon Schama, "the stereotype of the ugly American— voracious, preachy, mercenary, and bombastically chauvinist—was firmly in place in Europe."[18]

There is a special place in foreign news outlets for Americans who are displeased with their country's popular culture or their government's policies. The U.S. writers most often featured in the media covered by the Columbia journalism students' reports were U.S. critics Noam Chomsky and the late Edward Said. Chomsky, a professor at M.I.T., has appeared in *El Pais* (Spain), the *New Statesman* (United Kingdom), *La Jornada* (Mexico), and *Le Monde* (France); Said, a Columbia University professor, had appeared in *El Pais*, the *New Statesman*, *La Jornada*, and *Clarin* (Argentina). Even actor Woody Harrelson has appeared in the foreign press, writing "I'm an American tired of American lies," in the *Guardian*.[19] Martin Burcharth, U.S. correspondent for the left-of-center Danish daily *Information*, related how "[f]rom the first days of reporting on 9/11 in *Information*, it became clear to me that the editors and reporters pursuing the story from our Copenhagen office almost exclusively sought out those Americans, Europeans, and Arabs who espoused the line: The U.S. had it coming."[20]

The United States does, nonetheless, have supporters. There were widely reprinted articles supporting U.S. intervention in Afghanistan by Italian journalist Oriana Fallaci, whose commentary first appeared in *Corriere Della Sera* and was reprinted in *O Independenta* (Portugal) and *La Nacion* (Argentina). But as Fahd Hussain said of the Pakistani press, at the same time a "deep-seated mistrust of the U.S. bubbled up to the surface." In one of the most virulently anti-American articles, Antonio Caballero, described by one of the Columbia students as "perhaps the most respected journalist in Colombia," wrote:

> It was only natural that after a half century of the American
> government devastating cities around the world—Tokyo,
> Dresden, Hiroshima, Korean villages, Hanoi, Beirut, Panama,
> Tripoli, Kabul, Baghdad, Belgrade—it would be New York

and Washington's turn to experience horror. They have spent their whole lives sowing rancor through the world; they should not be surprised now by what they are reaping.[21]

From London in 2002, T. R. Reid, of the *Washington Post,* summarized what the America of the Bush era looked like in the British media:

Americans are crass, crude and insular. They worship the handgun and the electric chair in equal measure. They pollute the planet, bomb innocent civilians and force unwilling consumers everywhere to buy their overpriced running shoes and oversize hamburgers. They even managed to wreck the Winter Olympics with all their whooping, flag-waving and yew-ess-saying.

That's the picture of our country painted by the British media, where columns of America-bashing are as common as the daily weather forecast and the cricket scores. "The one issue that all the papers agree on, from far left to far right," notes Michael Gove, assistant editor of the *London Times,* "is anti-Americanism."[22]

National Interests

Ultimately, each country's media assess how U.S. policies and actions fit into the contours of its own national interests. After 9/11, India's press saw implications for the geopolitics of the subcontinent in the U.S.-Afghan conflict. The *Hindustan Times* speculated on "how 'fair' Washington will be to India given that it's now allied with Pakistan."[23] The events of 9/11 affected the Philippines too, in terms of the Abu Sayyaf and the country's Muslim insurgency problem. For Yasemin Congar, Washington bureau chief of the Turkish newspaper *Milliyet,* Turkey's "national interest" in late 2001 related to whether the war in Afghanistan might expand to Iraq, which borders Turkey. For Jose Carreno, Washington bureau chief for Mexico City's *El Universal,* one important aspect of the "war on terrorism" was "the U.S. borders with Mexico, in terms of vigilance, in terms of trade, in terms of immigration, in terms of the people that are already here, illegal aliens."[24]

The international flow of news is asymmetrical. The United States pays far less attention to other countries than other countries pay to the United States. "The United States is a source of more absorbing fascination to Europeans than ever an individual European country could be to the United States," said Foreign Secretary Jack Straw of Britain in 2002.[25] Year after year, studies have illustrated the asymmetry: 50 percent of foreign news in Canada (1978) and in Japan (1987) was about the United States; Latin American papers (1961) had twenty times more news about the United States than U.S. papers had about Latin America.[26] One can blame the ignorance and arrogance of Americans. Or the selfishness of their news organizations. But viewed another way, the disparity simply reflects the reality of America's place in today's world.

Then

What we know about foreign correspondents in America, 1955–88

The 111 responses to a questionnaire that graduate student Donald A. Lambert mailed to 250 foreign correspondents in the United States in 1955 provide a benchmark against which later surveys can be compared. His survey documented a group of predominantly male (there were only six women), well-educated (fifteen had doctoral degrees), experienced journalists in their mid-forties who did mostly interpretive reporting. They mailed more than half of their articles back to the home office and sent another 27 percent by cable. They seemed to like Americans. When the correspondents were asked to check the adjectives that they considered most descriptive, ninety-three voted for "friendly," ninety for "generous," and eighty-seven for "peace-loving." There were twenty-eight check marks for "bad-mannered" and one for "lazy."[1]

Twenty years later another investigation found a foreign press corps that was growing rapidly, up from 250 to 865 correspondents, but that looked about the same in terms of demographic and professional characteristics. More than half were from Western Europe (465), with Asia next (132, of whom 82 reported for Japan), followed by Latin America (77) and the Middle East (53, of whom 23 were from Israel).[2] There were four correspondents from sub-Saharan Africa in 1977, two representing the Ghana News Agency, one from the Ivory Coast, and another who divided her time among French language papers in several African countries.[3]

Canada received an assessment of its own in 1978 when a student at Carleton University interviewed the fifteen correspondents representing the Canadian media in Washington. "The myths and romance surrounding the 'Foreign Correspondent' seem inapplicable to the Canadian correspondents working in Washington," began Lorna Bratvold's article. "With perhaps the exception of the Quebecois correspondents, the Canadian correspondents do not view themselves as foreign correspondents." Most of her interviewees wrote articles with a Canadian angle. Ben Tierney of the Southam newspapers commented, "There are essentially two kinds of stories down here as far as the Canadians are concerned. The first is 'Oh, look, they're shitting on us again,' when the Americans do something bad. . . . And the other is, if they're giving something to us, it's 'Oh, they're paying attention to us.' "[4]

My own research began in 1979, with eighty-seven interviews conducted in Washington with journalists from thirty countries.[5] After each correspondent had talked for approximately fifteen minutes, the English proficiency of the fifty-four subjects from non–English-speaking countries was rated on a scale of 1 to 5. Fifty-two percent spoke excellent English; 24 percent, fair; and 24 percent, poor. There was no geographic pattern. Those at the bottom came from Czechoslovakia, Denmark, Guatemala, Israel, Japan, and Spain. However, of those who had been in the United States for two years or less, five of eight were rated "poor." There were measurable improvements when we "retested" them three years later. Almost all the correspondents from non–English-speaking countries indicated that their reading ability was superior to their speaking ability.

Perhaps our most unusual finding in 1979 related to what correspondents worried about. Twenty-three percent said that it was having "too much information," an odd problem for a journalist. Could too much information be more of a disadvantage than too little information? Perhaps it could, if a deadline was approaching and a reporter lacked the knowledge to select sources wisely. Comparing U.S. government information policies to those in other countries, Harold Jackson of the *Guardian* (United Kingdom) noted in 1979, "I think you have the best Official Secrets Act. You simply pour it all out. No one could possibly keep up with it."[6] Too much information was primarily a problem of correspondents who were newly arrived in Washington: it was cited by 54 percent of those who had been there for less than three years, by 38 percent of those based there between three and five years, by 8 percent of those based there between five and ten years, and by no correspondent with more than ten years' experience in the city.

In 1979 our correspondents averaged thirty-three days of work-related travel a year, visiting twenty-nine states overall. That was higher than the number of days reported in previous studies, an increase that might have been a by-product of the dollar's decline—the United States was a bargain at the time. Collectively, the eighty-seven Washington-based reporters made ten or more trips to eight states: New York (thirty-nine trips), California (thirty-three), Illinois (nineteen), Texas (twelve), Florida (eleven), Pennsylvania (eleven), Massachusetts (ten), and Georgia (ten). Georgia was the home of President Jimmy Carter, while the NASA space program had centers in Texas and Florida. Respondents rarely took trips away from the East or West Coast and almost always traveled to large cities.[7] "Not many seek contact with Midwestern America," wrote American journalist Thomas Littlewood. "Still fewer venture into the South. In the main, therefore, they don't see and talk to Americans who dine at McDonald's, bowl on Tuesday evenings, attend the stock car races, guzzle beer at the Legion hall, or shoot baskets in a ghetto schoolyard."[8]

Paradoxically, it was the presidential nominating system, unloved by scholars, that regularly sent reporters to smaller states and small towns that they would not otherwise have visited. Tom Swinson, a program officer at the U.S. government's Foreign Press Centers, described taking a busload to Hampstead, New Hampshire, during the 1980 primary:

> It was really something. Reagan is talking to this group
> when suddenly this bus pulls up and about 40 foreign cor-
> respondents jump out and start asking him questions. We
> outnumbered everyone else. Here Reagan was, speaking infor-
> mally with some citizens and local reporters one minute,
> and then the next minute he is being asked some difficult
> foreign policy questions by reporters from Peking. And this
> is in Hampstead.

In 1983, another survey of Washington-based foreign correspondents, by graduate student Shailendra Ghorpade, showed graphically how reporters were changing the way that they transmit stories. Instead of relying on regular mail as they had in Lambert's 1955 study, 38 percent were now using "satellite links, telephone-linked word processors, and facsimile." Ghorpade also started to quantify foreign correspondents' reliance on "borrowed news." More than presidential press con-

ferences, State Department or embassy briefings, or interviews with
diplomats or legislators, the journalists' primary sources were "U.S.
newspapers."[9] It is not a habit unique to foreign correspondents in the
United States. Concluded British media researcher David Morrison, "A
rule of foreign reporting [is] that a correspondent is as good as the local
media."[10]

Scholars' early studies are helpful in suggesting trends. However,
the applicability of their results is shaky because of small sample sizes,
low response rates, and problems with the lists from which the sam-
ples were drawn.

There were also a number of lengthy newspaper and magazine articles about foreign correspondents during the 1972–1986 period that
tended to profile individual correspondents, helping to explain what
life was like in the foreign press corps. Those portraits suggested that
not all correspondents were valued equally in the Oval Office and
Georgetown drawing rooms.

At the top of the pecking order were the British, with their "special
relationship" to government officials and the upper echelons of
society—or, at least, members of their elite press, such as correspondents from the *Times,* the *Telegraph,* and the *Guardian* and the BBC's
Alistair Cooke, who had been doing a weekly "Letter from America"
radio essay since 1946. They tended to be Oxford or Cambridge men.
"The BBC chief correspondent [in Washington] and the two *Observer*
correspondents all attended the same Cambridge college," wrote
British journalist Patrick Brogan. "Of the four *Times* chief correspondents since 1970, three went to Cambridge, one to Oxford."[11] (Cooke,
the son of a metalworker, attended Jesus College, Cambridge.)[12]

A modest irony was that the best connected—and some would say
most English—of this elite club was not of the Oxbridge set. Henry
Brandon, of the *Sunday Times,* was a Czech émigré who had fled to England when his country was invaded by Germany. In 1974 Sam Lipski,
who covered Washington for the *Australian,* recalled his first conversation with Brandon: "Radcliffe [Lipski's name for Brandon's secretary]
came in, apologized for the interruption, but explained it was 'Mr.
McNamara calling.' Brandon picked up the phone and said: 'Bob! How
are you? Where were you last week? I missed you at Chamonix.' "
(Robert McNamara, former secretary of defense, was then president of
the World Bank.)[13]

Another breed of British correspondent approached the Washington scene with a more irreverent air. The extreme example was one

James Gibson, sent to Washington in 1978 by the *Daily Mail*, who soon was fabricating stories about "beggars in bowlers" outside the White House, Secret Service agents getting President Carter's lunch from Loeb's Deli on Fifteenth Street, Richard Nixon planning to crash a NATO summit to promote his book, and ultimately (before Gibson was finally returned to London) Carter's advisers proposing that the president counter his sagging image by growing an Abe Lincoln beard.[14]

Soviet journalists also interested the American press, but for a special reason. "TASS: Is It a News Agency or Spy Network?" ran a headline in the *Lowell* (Mass.) *Sun* in 1982. The story offered an answer: "Federal officials believe TASS [the Telegraph Agency of the Soviet Union] reporters do more spying than reporting." While no Soviet correspondents were expelled from the United States, five were expelled from Britain in 1985. In tit-for-tat travel restrictions, the State Department banned Soviet journalists from about 20 percent of the country and prohibited them from getting within twenty-five miles of any military establishment. Lamented Anatoly Manakov of *Literaturnaya Gazeta*, "The dream of my life in the United States is not going to be fulfilled, and that is to be in Disney World."[15] The same travel restrictions applied to journalists from the People's Republic of China.[16]

Feature articles about the foreign press corps in *Editor and Publisher* (1960), the *Saturday Review* (1972), the *Washington Post* (1979), the *Washington Journalism Review* (1980), and the *National Journal* (1985) collectively painted a picture of "haves" and "have nots." The latter were small operations, mostly one-person bureaus. "Forced to make a choice of one city where they can keep their eyes on America," observed the author of a 1960 report, "the vast majority of foreign newsmen choose New York," commute to Washington, and have limited funds available for other travel.[17]

At the bottom of the pecking order were the part-time correspondents, those who cobbled together an income by writing articles for publications in their home country while doing other kinds of work, often translating and interpreting. "If mine were a rich paper," wrote Wilson Velloso, a Brazilian journalist in Washington, "I wouldn't have to do anything else. But it isn't, so I am thankful to be able to work as a linguist." After doing a story about NASA's Venus explorations, he turned to interpreting "for a couple who come to see an orthopedist" about their daughter's medical problems.[18]

Many profiles of foreign correspondents suggested that coming to the United States was an end in itself. "To be sent to Washington is the most prestigious assignment a Japanese correspondent can receive," said a bureau chief for *Asahi Shimbun*.[19] Max Boot of Switzerland's *Neue Zurcher Zeitung*, seventy-four years old in 1960, had covered all forty-seven annual meetings of the UN General Assembly. Indeed, some foreign correspondents had become American citizens.

Correspondents posted in America during this period seemed to agree with Barber's axiom, reporting that they were indeed very happy that their home offices paid little attention to them. The Washington correspondent for *Peskor*, South Africa's largest newspaper, said, "Sometimes two weeks [in 1979] will pass without my calling my office."[20] Many also claimed, as did Marino de Medici of the Italian newspaper *Il Tempo*, that "compared with most other capitals, Washington offers easy access to information, even for foreign correspondents."[21] Wrote the political editor of the BBC, "The great eye-opener for a British journalist who works in Washington is the apparently instinctive openness of government and politics there contrasted with our [the United Kingdom's] instinctive privacy."[22] Another British journalist, Marc Ross of the *Daily Express*, told an interviewer in 1982, "The foreign press is spoiled rotten when it comes to access in Washington."[23] Not all agreed. Complained one "have not," Edmund Lachman of Holland's *NRC Handelsblad*:

> Except for [Werner] Imhoof [of *Neue Zurcher Zeitung*] and some of the socially elite British representatives, Washington is a disaster area for foreign correspondents. We are treated like total dirt at the State Department or Henry Kissinger's [National Security Council] office. It took me months to make an appointment with one of Kissinger's assistants. During the interview he was quite bored and made it clear that he did not expect me to come back. Why? Because this is a government interested mainly in being reelected, and we don't represent any votes.[24]

In the opinion of Jean-Francois Lisee, correspondent for a French language Montreal daily, "If you can't prove that actual-real-important-American voters read your stuff, you might as well be a potted plant."[25] It was the rare foreign correspondent who agreed with John Edwards of the *Australian Bulletin*, who told us in 1982, "One has to concede that not talking to foreign correspondents is somewhat of a rational use of time."

To attempt any study of the movements of foreign correspondents is like trying to "nail currant jelly to the wall" (to use a favorite expression of Theodore Roosevelt's). The normal ebb and flow could be seen in Washington from 1979 to 1982: Australia's *National Times* closed its bureau so that it could open a new one in Tokyo; EFE, the Spanish news agency, expanded from three to five correspondents; the bureau chief for Deutsche Presse-Agentur opted to take the bureau chief's job in Bonn; a Canadian correspondent left to "have babies in Philadelphia"; Herbert von Borch, of *Suddeutsche Zeitung*, retired, and Stephen Barber died; revolution closed the office of Kayhan Newspapers Tehran; and sixteen journalists departed because of their organization's rotation policies.

An overarching impression that emerges from these 1955–88 accounts of foreign correspondents is that the United States was a comfortable place to live and work, although it could be a difficult place to explain. "The reality of how a President and other political leaders obtain and exercise power is so complicated," mused Adalbert de Segonzac of *France Soir*.[26] A correspondent for *Hurrivet*, a Turkish newspaper, concurred: "Electoral colleges, primaries, and caucuses are so complicated, only an academic could understand." And, having just returned from a Foreign Press Center excursion to the New Hampshire primary in 1984, Ode Okore, a Nigerian reporter, said that he could not understand why Gary Hart had to field those touchy questions about his marriage: "In my country if a politician goes through all the women in a village, he is proud of it."[27] The United States was complicated.

WHO
THEY ARE

"After I graduated from university, I just went to this company [and] got a job. I joined this company [in] 1989. Once you join a newspaper company, most are supposed to work [for the company] until retirement. It's very stable. . . . Before coming here, I belonged to the foreign news department. . . . before that, from 1996 to 1998, I was the Hong Kong correspondent and I cover[ed] the handover of Hong Kong from Britain. Before that, from 1994 to 1995, I studied [the] Chinese language, a sort of foreign language program [paid for] by my company. . . . So [the] company wanted[ed] me to be kind of a China hand. My boss tried to send me [to] Beijing or Washington. Maybe later I'm supposed to be a Beijing correspondent. But he decided it's better for me [and] for the company to make a China hand who knows U.S. foreign policy very well also."

—Nobu Sakajiri, *Asahi Shimbun* (Japan),
July 11, 2002

"I started my journalism [career] when I met [*name inaudible*], who was living in the Congo for a very, very long time and had been successful in business there. He was kind of an advocate for people who [immigrated] there. [He started the] magazine *L'émigré*. It focuses on immigrants' issues. The Senegalese are everywhere these days. They are world travelers, and these issues are very important. So he came back to Senegal and decided to do something to give back. [He asked me if] I would go to the United States and be a kind of correspondent. . . . I worked a little bit in Senegal just before coming here. Three months, and then I came here."

—Ibru Wane, *L'émigré* (Senegal),
August 10, 2002

"In 1958 someone told me to apply for [an] associate Neiman fellowship at Harvard. . . . So I went to Harvard for a year. . . . At the end of the year, the last three months, they

weren't really interested in the United States in India. We had
interest in [the] United Nations because we were a member
and the speeches there were really important. . . . So they said,
'Why don't you go to the UN for three months?' . . . And after
three months, they asked me if I could stay another three
months. . . . I told my wife, 'You better come along. They said
three months, [but] I don't know how long it is going to be.' . . .
After three years, the largest paper in India told me I could
work for them and get a byline and weekly column. . . . And for
twenty years I did that. . . . The PTI said, 'We have no correspondent in Washington, why don't you work in Washington?' . . . So now I've been in this country for forty-two years."

—T. V. Parasuram, Press Trust of India,
August 29, 2002

"Everyone wants to be a foreign correspondent in the U.S. . . .
It's very competitive. I'm also fortunate to be the first female
Chinese journalist ever in D.C., I mean from the mainland. And
second, I'm the youngest ever, twenty-seven years old. [*Phone
rings.*] That's probably my editor. Do you mind? . . . There is still
a concept [in China] that female correspondents [are] kind of
weak. They are sent to small countries, easy place[s]."

—Wei Tian, China Radio International,
August 18, 2002

"Needless to say, when I was in fifth grade, I already knew that
I wanted to be a journalist. Wrote for *Pioneerskaya Pravda*, the
Pioneer journal. . . . And ever since then, I had no change of
mind in what I wanted to become, although a few times there,
under the influence of various amorous stories, I wanted to be
a geologist. . . . In 1993 I happened to come here not knowing
a nick of English because my wife got a job at the World
Bank. . . . I worked for *Delovoi Mir* at that period. . . . It was
hard at first not knowing the language. I still know it poorly,
but understand it—the written text I started to comprehend
early on, knowing French. When this newspaper ceased to exist,
the magazine *Itogi* remained. . . . My wife got bored here, and
she left for Moscow, works in Moscow now. As for me, after
suffering for many years I got used to it, and consider that for
a foreign journalist there is no work like the one I do."

—Nickolay Zimin, *Itogi* (Russia),
November 18, 2003

Patterns

Some findings, 1999–2003

The foreign press corps in the United States experienced a growth spurt in the second half of the twentieth century, from 616 correspondents in 1964 to more than three times that number in 2000, according to the *Editor and Publisher International Year Book.*[1] The biggest increase was in the number of reporters from Asia, whose share of the press corps rose from 17 to 27 percent. But all regions gained, even underrepresented Africa, whose contingent increased from seven to thirty-three correspondents. Yet Western Europe, with 47 percent, still dominated. Growth was especially robust in the 1990–2000 period, when, ironically, U.S. news organizations were sharply reducing their international coverage.[2] (See figure 1, page 30.)

New York City—the country's cultural hub and home to Wall Street and the UN—was reported to be the primary location of foreign journalists in 1998.[3] But in 1999, when we had enough information to divide the press corps into full-time and part-time correspondents, we found a different pattern. A larger percentage of the full-timers lived in Washington; a larger percentage of the part-timers lived in New York.[4] Ninety-eight countries had correspondents posted in the United States in 1999; fifty-five countries had correspondents in both Washington and New York; thirty-two had correspondents only in Washington, and eleven had correspondents only in New York. Increasingly, it was as a political power that the United States was attracting the world's media.

The expansion of the foreign press corps also reflected television's coming of age. While the number of foreign correspondents who were members of the Congressional Press Galleries grew nearly

FIGURE 1. Foreign Correspondents in the United States, by
Place of Origin, 2000

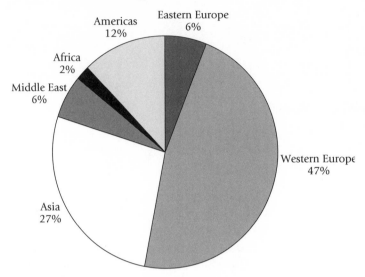

Source: *Editor and Publisher International Year Book.*

eight times between 1961 and 2002 (from 110 to 860), those reporting for television multiplied twenty-four times (figure 2, page 31). The BBC and Reuters TV opened major bureaus in Washington, German and Japanese television were well represented, and even small countries—Switzerland, Denmark, Holland, Finland—established a permanent television presence in the capital.[5]

In Washington the downtown center of foreign press activity is the National Press Building, where the government maintains one of its three Foreign Press Centers. There is a private press club on the top floor, and some news organizations are headquartered there, notably Japanese and Korean newspapers and a number of the smaller wire services, such as ANSA (Italy), Notimex (Mexico), and ITAR-TASS (Russia). In New York City there are the UN delegate lounges, where members of the press can meet, and the Foreign Press Center on East 52nd Street. But a spectrogram of foreign correspondents in Washington or New York would show an array of one-person bureaus, with many journalists working out of their homes in Silver Spring, Arlington, Bethesda, and Takoma Park—or Forrest Hills, Woodside, Teaneck, and Brooklyn—or, for the better subsidized, Georgetown or Sutton Place. (See

FIGURE 2. Foreign Press Corps Members of the Congressional Press
Galleries, by Medium

Number of members

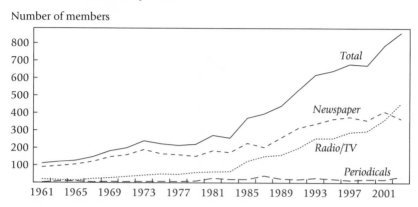

Source: Congressional Directory.

table 1, page 42, for the number of foreign correspondents accredited
by the Foreign Press Centers in 2003).

The office of Pierre Steyn, correspondent for National Media of
South Africa, was windowless, "a glorified broom closet on the
eleventh floor of the National Press Building, just large enough to
house a desk and an armchair and little else," reported my research
assistant, Daniel Reilly, in 2002; it was "smaller than my college dorm-
room." Moreover, it contained "the oldest computer I had ever seen,
and a TV so old it had UHF settings." In stark contrast, at the office of
the *Economist* (United Kingdom), on Pennsylvania Avenue between
the White House and the Capitol, there were leather chairs and flat-
screen TVs. Here a visitor was immediately impressed with photographs of George H. W. Bush aboard Air Force One (reading the
Economist) and George W. Bush aboard Air Force One (reading
the *Economist*).

A half-hour taxi ride from the *Economist*'s office was the apartment
complex in suburban Maryland where Tomasz Zalewski of the Polish
Press Agency lived and worked. Stacks of newspapers and clippings
lined his hallway and walls. CNN was on in every room. His employer
paid for the apartment and a car, which, he said, "I don't so much use,
actually." He went downtown only "twice a week on average." He sub-
scribed to the Federal News Service for transcripts of White House and
State Department briefings and relied on newspapers and the Internet,
some personal contacts, and the people at the Foreign Press Center to

produce "about twenty to twenty-five stories a week." He and his wife had "more Polish friends than American. That's common. Our Polish friends, they also have more Polish friends than American."[6] His life was not exactly that of the "Foreign Correspondent" as played by Gregory Peck in *Roman Holiday*.

The five-page questionnaire that we sent to foreign correspondents in 1999 asked for information on age, sex, citizenship, employer, years in journalism, years as a correspondent in the United States, experience (if any) as a student in the United States, last post before coming to the United States, work not related to journalism, number and type of stories reported each week, relations with the home office, travel, countries covered in addition to the United States, language fluency, freelance work, media reading and listening habits, Internet use, use of the Foreign Press Centers, and access to sources (see figure 3, page 33). It also asked open-ended questions about job frustrations, aspects of their job that they enjoyed, and advice on improving coverage of the United States.

The responses indicated that the "average" full-time foreign correspondent in the United States was a forty-two-year-old man. (There were three men for every woman.) The median number of years that he had been in the United States was four. It had been two years since he was last in his home country. He wrote nine stories a week; seven were hard news, two were features, and two mentioned his country (the home angle). He read four daily newspapers and *Time* or *Newsweek*, listened to National Public Radio, and spent nearly three hours a day on the Internet.[7] Eighty percent of the correspondents considered themselves proficient in English; only 1 percent used an interpreter. Nearly half of the correspondents had some responsibility for covering countries besides the United States, such as Canada (19 percent), Latin America (14 percent), Mexico (11 percent), or Cuba (7 percent).

The portrait that emerged was of a well-educated cadre; advanced degrees, some earned in the United States or Britain, were quite common. "NHK [a Japanese TV network] sent me to the Tufts University graduate school, from 1998 to 1999, for one year," said Takeshi Yamashita. "NHK is very generous. Of course, they pay for my education. So I studied international relations there. It's a mid-career program so you can get [an] M.A. in one year. And then after the university, I came to Washington [to be a] correspondent."[8] Doctorates appeared on several resumes: Moroccan Abderrahim Foukara, Al Jazeera, had a Ph.D. in African literature from Glasgow University; Egyptian

FIGURE 3. Characteristics of Full-Time Correspondents, 1999[a]

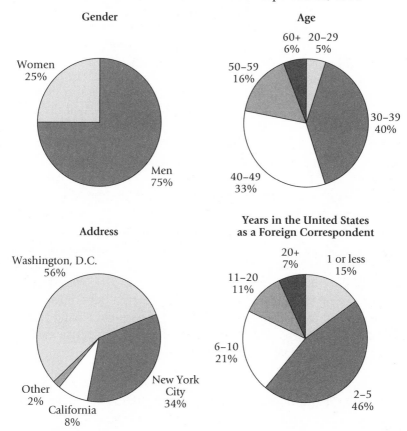

a. Number of respondents: gender = 350; age = 307; address = 349; years = 343.

Mohammed Said, *Al-Ahram*, had a Ph.D. in political science from the University of North Carolina at Chapel Hill.

Very few correspondents had studied journalism, although several had come to the United States to enter a journalism program, and others noted that it is now more common to major in journalism than it was when they were students. Tom Buhrow, Washington bureau chief for German television network ARD-TV, noted:

> At the time I went to college in Germany, from 1978 through 1984, the journalism schools were more theoretical. It was more the academic examination of journalism. It was not the trade. You didn't learn the trade, number one. And point two,

the guys who were in charge, the editors, were basically a self-taught generation and didn't think a lot about theory. So it was not an advantage to go to journalism school. [No one thought], "Oh, I want to become a journalist. I'm going to go into journalism school." Journalism schools weren't what they are today in Germany.[9]

European survey respondents tended to have studied the social sciences; Asians were more interested in learning languages. "I'm a student of [the] English language," said Rujun Wang, of China. "So they need these kinds of skills. So I worked for *People's Daily* as a correspondent."[10]

Another Chinese correspondent, Yan Feng, Xinhua News Agency, told us, "My parents are almost illiterate. When I was very young, because China was a communist country, school [was] free for everyone. A lot of people in China come from very poor families. I had no journalism experience, but I studied very hard English in my university."[11] In general, however, the correspondents' background of university training and previous independent foreign travel suggest that they belonged to the upper social classes. Explained Chang Choi of MBC-TV (Korea), who was a German major in South Korea and later got an M.P.A. from Harvard's Kennedy School of Government:

Korean journalists, comparatively, are from more wealthy families than [journalists in] the United States because in our development period the journalist [had] a great role in setting [up] the democratic system. Lots of journalists transfer in Korea from [the] journalistic field to [the] political arena. A journalist became prime minister."12

Takeshi Yamashita, the NHK correspondent, was the son of a banker and did his undergraduate degree in law:

It's a kind of cultural choice. In Japan, we don't have many schools for journalism. So in Japan a law degree is very, very popular. Most students who get a law degree don't go into a law area—lawyer, prosecutor or jurist. There are so few people because [the] Japanese bar exam is very, very difficult. So many people [are dissuaded]. I wanted to [be a] journalist, and I didn't want to be a lawyer, but to know law is a good [preparation for journalism].

Mike Hayashi, of *Yomiuri Shimbun*, also got a law degree. "Few Japanese have journalism degrees that go into journalism because there are not many journalism schools, but lots of newspapers."[13]

There was an element of randomness to some correspondents' choice of career. Said Ennino Carreto of *Corriere Della Sera:*

> The reason I became a foreign correspondent is because when
> I was in college in Italy, in Turin, I wanted to see England.
> That was the '60s. That was a time of great changes in Great
> Britain and the Beatles [were popular]. So I went there, and I
> went to London School of Economics. I found out that I
> could stay there only if I kept myself, and the only way I
> could keep myself was by writing. So I began writing. I began
> sending stories to Italian newspapers.[14]

Jorge Banales, EFE News Service (Spain), reported: "I was exiled from my country [Uruguay] to Buenos Aires and there was an opening for a translator at Reuters. They needed someone who was bilingual."[15] Henry Champ, Canadian Broadcasting Company: "I was a student of moderate achievement, but I was a good athlete. A local newspaper, upon my departure from the university, offered me a job in the sports department. I had never had the slightest thought ever about journalism."[16] Julian Borger, the *Guardian:* "I came to it as an economist in Africa, when I became a journalist and switched professions. [It was] a little less boring than being an economist."[17]

Consider the classical model of the foreign correspondent— Stanley Washburn, for example. Between 1904 and 1917, Washburn reported on a hundred battles and three wars for the *Chicago Daily News* and *Collier's Weekly.* He was with Baron Nogi at Port Arthur in the Russo-Japanese War and with the French at Verdun, traveling the world with his saddle, for "on a hurry call that may mean days of riding . . . [and it could make] all the difference between success and failure."[18] Or the Polish journalist Ryszard Kapuscinski. In 1966, having already witnessed twenty-seven revolutions in the third world, Kapuscinski was in Nigeria to cover a civil war: "I was driving along a road where they say no white man can come back alive. I am driving to see if a white man could, because I had to experience everything for myself."[19] Foreign correspondence, simply defined, was the work of full-time journalists who were posted away from their home country almost permanently. They were usually wanderers, although some were specialists who remained in a particular country or region.

That pattern could still be found in the foreign press corps in the United States in the late 1990s. *Times of India* correspondent Ramesh Chandran had been stationed in Paris for five years, reassigned to London for five years, and then sent back to Delhi to be foreign editor for five years before being posted to Washington.[20] Agustin Remesal (Spain) had come to Washington in 1999 from a tour in Paris; Morgan Olofsson (Sweden) and Bert Lanting (Holland) had come from Moscow; Carlos Fino (Portugal) and Michael Ulveman (Denmark) had come from Brussels; and Gilles Senges (France) and Thomas Knipp (Germany) had come from London.

From the employer's perspective, the question of how long to keep a correspondent in a country is a matter of personnel management (giving good people a crack at prestige assignments), expense (the cost of moving correspondents and their families), correspondents' personal needs (what is best for their children and spouses), and the fit of a specific correspondent to a particular post (language skills and previous experience in a country). We asked rotating correspondents to pick an ideal number of years to be in the United States—a golden mean between the time that it takes to learn the territory and the time that the assignment begins to grow stale. Especially for those in Washington, a presidential term, four years, was about right.

Our 1999 survey, however, suggested that the classical model was not the wave of the future. The configuration of the full-time foreign press corps was as follows: 52 percent came directly from the home office (although some had previous experience as foreign correspondents); 20 percent were local hires; and 12 percent were freelancers. Only 16 percent had been rotated from another foreign assignment.

Many of those who came directly from the home office had worked on the foreign desk, to which they would probably return. Others were rising stars—a TV anchor, diplomatic correspondent, foreign editor—who wanted a U.S. tour to buff their image. "After six years in Washington, Yoshihisa Komori is now considered the George Will of newspaper columnists in Japan," wrote Clyde Farnsworth in the *New York Times*.[21]

For organizations anxious to cut costs, the expense of transporting foreign correspondents—and their families—from post to post around the world can be avoided by tapping the endless supply of American journalists who are available as "local hires" or of full-time freelancers offering their services for more modest fees. Best of all are Italian Americans or Japanese Americans or Polish Americans or others who can report back to their country of origin.

Of the 410 correspondents who answered our questions about citizenship, more than one in five said that they were Americans, including nine with dual citizenship. Of greater significance, nearly 15 percent of the full-timers, those who usually work for the major news outlets, were U.S. citizens. The full-timers who were citizens were divided almost equally between native-born and naturalized citizens. Most prominent of the expatriates was Alistair Cooke, born near Manchester, England, in 1908, who moved to New York to report for the BBC in 1937 and became an American citizen in 1941. His last broadcast—on issues shaping the presidential election—aired on February 20, 2004. He died the following month, having been a Yank for almost twice as long as he had been a Brit.[22]

In short, more foreign correspondents in the United States were U.S. citizens than were Japanese citizens (12 percent) or German citizens (11 percent), the two next-largest groups (figure 4, page 38).

In addition, many foreign bureaus employ Americans as support staff, although they are not included in our computations. For instance, in 1998 the Washington bureau of *Nikkei-Nihon Keizai Shimbun* had eight Japanese correspondents and two American staff members, one to deal with economics and politics and the other a specialist in computer technology and information systems.[23] Rudiger Lentz, Washington bureau chief of German TV network Deutsche Welle, described his operation in 2002:

> I have a television studio with twelve people working for me; three are Americans—two technicians and one administration person. They are also sources, because they are plain people; they are coming in the morning and they have seen the news, but maybe they perceived the news in a different way than I did, and we talk about it. . . . So I want them to be part of the decision process, the building of my own opinion."[24]

Because of opportunities or circumstances, an unprecedented number of Americans are working as foreign correspondents in their own country. Jim Anderson, Milwaukee-born, was the UPI's State Department reporter for fifteen years. In late 1990 he switched to cover

FIGURE 4. Citizenship of Full-Time Foreign Correspondents[a]

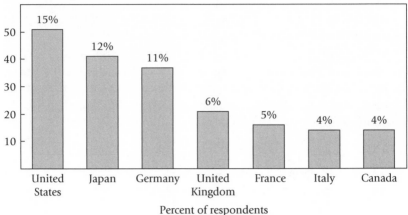

Number of respondents

Percent of respondents

a. Number of respondents = 344.

the State Department for Deutsche Presse-Agentur (DPA). Why the switch? "I had to leave UPI because it was too depressing to see what was happening to a great organization. . . . It was losing money, people, influence, losing everything. It's just, it's hollow," he told us in 2002, adding that he had "had a very pleasant eleven years with DPA."[25] When we first learned of Peter Ennis in 1999, he was a forty-two-year-old New Yorker who had become a foreign correspondent specializing in economic news without leaving home. At the time he was editor of the *Oriental Economist,* an English language publication of Toyo Keizai, and a correspondent for *Weekly Toyo Keizai.* He said that he planned to stay in the United States and assume increased management responsibilities within the paper over time. Checking back five years later, we found that he had remained in New York as contributing editor of the *Oriental Economist* and U.S. bureau chief of *Weekly Toyo Keizai.*[26]

A number of American journalists became stay-at-home foreign correspondents by working for the *Jerusalem Post* or the *Jerusalem Report,* Israeli publications published in English. CNN anchor Wolf Blitzer began his career in 1972 in Reuters' Tel Aviv bureau, then went to Washington for fifteen years with the *Jerusalem Post.* In 1987 he told *National Journal,* "I'm an American Jew who writes for an Israeli newspaper. I'm not an Israeli, but I speak Hebrew."²⁷ He joined CNN in 1990 as its Pentagon correspondent. Another American, Janine Zacharia, who was the *Jerusalem Post*'s Washington correspondent when she was interviewed in 2002, also started as a reporter in Israel after college. "I took a nontraditional route. Most people start at a local newspaper and try and work their way up. I'm trying to work my way back to a mid-sized American paper. . . . I guess I'm being a big shot. I cover the biggest story in the world."²⁸ (In March, 2005, Zacharia switched to Bloomberg News, where she reports on diplomatic matters and the State Department.)

Dual citizenship usually indicated that the correspondent had one parent who was an American and one who was not, as in the case of Olivier Knox, of Agence France-Presse in Washington:

> My father is American, my mother is French, and I grew up half in France, half in the United States, bouncing back and forth, two years in the states, two years in France. I was born in Vermont [where his parents were professors at Middlebury College.] That meant that I was forever explaining one country [or] the other to my classmates and sometimes to grown-ups. Working for AFP . . . feels like an extension of that because I'm writing mostly for foreign audiences.

Betty Brannan Jaen, Washington correspondent for *La Prensa*, a daily newspaper in Panama, said: "I'm half Panamanian, half American. I was born in Boston, but grew up in Panama. I married someone I met in college in Boston."

How did Knox and Brannan Jaen think of themselves? Knox said that he was "a half foreigner" but then concluded, "I'm essentially an American correspondent working for a foreign agency. . . . I'm a lot more American than I am French now, a lot more."²⁹ In contrast, Brannan Jaen said: "I consider myself half-and-half. If there is a bigger half, it's the Panamanian half. When I write I always identify myself as a Panamanian."³⁰

When U.S.-born foreign correspondents in the United States were asked about any related journalistic advantages, they mentioned the way that they sound, their accent. Olivier Knox observed that "people you speak to here would rather hear an American voice on the phone than a deeply accented French voice [*said with a French accent*]. Simple fact. So you get treated differently." Janine Zacharia said, "Another reason why I have access over other Israeli or Arab media is because I'm American. So they can talk to me and trust me as an American. I don't have a thick accent."

Then there is what Jim Anderson said that "the Germans call the *fingerspitze*, the finger-tip feeling of the American scene." Recalling his years with DPA, he said, "They used me sort of as a sound board, as they do with the man who took my place. He's sort of the touchstone for the American culture." Olivier Knox's finger-tip example was alerting a disbelieving superior to how important reissuing the Star Wars movies was going to be. Lisa Lane, who worked for Japan's NHK-TV, said that she had a *fingerspitze* moment in 2002 when the Washington-area sniper forced schools to cancel homecoming activities: "What's homecoming? How does that translate? And what kind of cultural experience does that mean?"[31]

Naturalized foreign correspondents become U.S. citizens for the same reasons that have motivated immigrants throughout U.S. history. As a child, Sabine Reifenberg, of ARD-TV, fled the Nazis with her family. Her grandfather and father had been prominently associated with the *Frankfurter Allegemeine Zeitung*.[32] Many first came as students: Mohammad A. Salih, from Sudan, attended Indiana University; Mauro Calamandrei, from Italy, attended the University of Chicago; and Samir N. Nader, from Lebanon, went to California State University at Long Beach. Some fall in love and marry Americans. The CBC's Henry Champ: "I'm married to an American. I have American children. I have a farm and a house downtown. I'm here forever."[33] Long residency as a foreign correspondent can create its own dynamic, as noted by T. V. Parasuram, Press Trust of India:

> My son came to the United States when he was four. My daughter was born here. . . . So now, I've been in this country for forty-two years. Last August I said, I've spent more than half my life in this country and I [am still] renewing my visa every time. Then they changed the rules, and my family [all were] citizens, so I became a citizen.
>
> **Q:** *Do you still consider yourself an Indian even though you're an American citizen now?*
>
> **A:** Actually, I think that I am both of them. Just like anybody. . . . But if you asked me, "If there was a war, for whom would I fight?" I would fight for the United States.[34]

There was a difference in the responses of the foreign correspondents who chose to be Americans, an intensity that reflected the fact that they had earned their citizenship. Born in Beirut, Raghida Dergham became the New York correspondent for the Arabic daily *Al Hayat:*

> I think because I came to the United States when I was seventeen years old it taught me tremendously. Had I stayed in Beirut, I don't think I would have grown into the person I am now. In the States you have full freedom. So I put myself through college. I waited tables. I made submarine sandwiches. My uncle said, "What is the matter? Why can't you accept help?" And I said, "The matter is I need to know if I can do it alone." The United States was the key that would bring about my freedom, my independence—the life I imagined I would lead.[35]

TABLE 1. Foreign Correspondents Accredited by the Foreign Press
          Centers, July 2003

Country	Number of correspondents	Population (in millions)
Japan	170	128
Germany	126	82
United Kingdom	56	59
Korea	53	48
China	34	1,304
France	32	60
Canada	30	32
Russia	27	143
Spain	26	41
India	25	1,065
Netherlands	19	16
Brazil	18	178
Italy	18	57
Taiwan	18	23
Turkey	18	71
Mexico	16	103
Middle East, other	16	N/A
Argentina	24	38
Saudi Arabia	13	24
Africa, other	12	N/A
Denmark	12	5
Switzerland	12	7
Greece	11	11
Israel	11	6
Egypt	10	72
Hong Kong	10	7
Norway	10	5
Sweden	10	9
Finland	9	5
Poland	9	39
Pakistan	8	154
Qatar	8	0.6

Irregulars

The other foreign correspondents

When in 1999 we surveyed all those whose names appeared on various lists of foreign correspondents in the United States, our analysis showed that 20 percent—one in five—were not full-time journalists. These were the irregulars. "Irregular" is a word with multiple associations—an irregular shape, an irregular verb, an irregular shirt—used here in the old-fashioned military sense: the irregulars are the troops who belong to no organized military force.

To simply call them part-timers is to suggest that they are just like traditional foreign correspondents, except that they work less. Some do fit that description. Having reported from the United States from 1960 to 1987, Marino de Medici, for example, was considered the dean of foreign correspondents in Washington, but he slowed down afterward to become U.S. contributor to *Affari Estera*, an Italian foreign affairs journal.[1]

Some traditional journalists become irregulars following marriage. Pamela Glass, an American, began reporting part-time for a newspaper on the Indian Ocean island of Mauritius after having married a Mauritian executive at the World Bank. On April 13, 1999, she was covering two competing African trade bills in Congress. Glass previously had been a full-time Washington correspondent for the Ottaway Newspapers.[2] Freke Vuijst, a Dutch journalist and documentary producer, married an American noted for writing mystery thrillers that feature Elvis Presley; in 1999 she was based in Great Barrington, Massachusetts.[3]

Most irregulars, however, are different from traditional foreign correspondents (see figure 1, page 44, for data on age, gender,

FIGURE 1. Characteristics of Part-Time Correspondents, 1999[a]

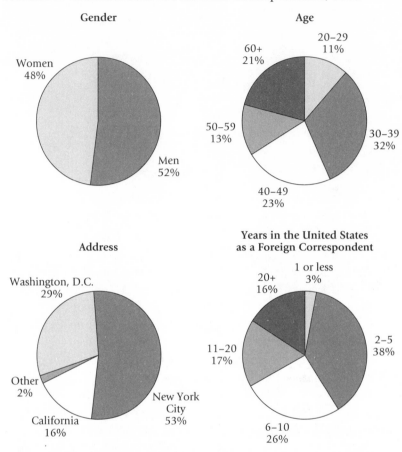

a. Number of respondents: gender = 89; age = 78; address = 89; years = 88.

address, and years as a correspondent in the United States). In part, of course, that is because they often do other things that are not related to journalism. Some work at the United Nations, the World Bank, or the Voice of America or for nongovernmental organizations. They may be translators or language teachers, or they may use their language skills in some other way. Charlie Torrini, an Argentine living in New York, spent half his time as a "court interpreter for Spanish-speaking defendants."[4] Spanish freelancer Montserrat Vendrell translated *Barron's How to Prepare for the GED*.[5] Adam A. Ouologuem, from Mali, said, "If you look at most of the African journalists here [in Washington], they are doing something else. Our president [of the African Correspondents Society] is a teacher in Montgomery County. So we are the ones struggling to make a living in this country."[6]

Our irregulars included graduate students and professors, artists and actors; among them were also an astrologist, a waitress, a Japanese trader in seafood, and a Chinese antique dealer. Gabriel Plesca, a Romanian novelist in New York, covered American literary life—from "Voices of the New Generation" to "Arthur Miller at Eighty"—for Bucharest magazines.[7] Monique Martens, a Belgian woman who spent half of her time in 1999 "trading the stock market," produced a story on the NBA finals for Dutch TV.[8]

The diversity among the irregulars was so great that a collective profile of them would merely be a collage of disparate backgrounds. Some arrived in the United States under dramatic circumstances. Elizabeth Mora-Mass fled Colombia to escape the wrath of Pablo Escobar. In 1986, after she wrote an article, "De Medallo a 'Metrallo' " ("From Medellin to 'Machine Gun City' "), she received an enraged phone call from the drug czar and knew that she was no longer safe in her country.[9] Jan Palarczyk feared persecution for his underground publications after the Polish government imposed martial law in 1982, and he was granted political asylum by the United States. He subsequently received a law degree and said that writing about freedom of speech was his favorite topic.[10]

Ibru Wane wrote about the immigrant community for a Senegal magazine. Interviewed at the dining room table in his Arlington, Virginia, apartment, amid leftover Spaghettios and empty cereal bowls, he explained, "I don't have a computer here, so I go to the library."[11] Edgardo Carlos Krebs, a Smithsonian Institution anthropologist from Argentina, was interviewed at a Library of Congress conference where he was speaking on the topic "How Do the Media, Popular Culture, and Literature Reflect National Character, Stereotypes, and Perceptions?" In 1999 he said that he wrote articles on the "Clinton controversies . . . typically with ethnographic or literary analysis."[12] Raj S. Rangarajan's articles—"Magic Bullets for Today's Man" and "Zen and the Art of Harley-Davidson"—appeared in *India Today Plus* (Your Guide to Good Living).[13] Barbara Probst Solomon was a professor in the graduate writing program at Sarah Lawrence College and cultural correspondent for *El Pais* (Madrid).[14]

Four irregulars listed their primary occupation as "marketing consultant," "specialist in international trade," owner of a "consulting practice that facilitates business links between the United States and Africa," or employee of a company whose website claimed that it "provides a comprehensive portfolio of confidential services." Their stories suggested that editors need to be alert to potential conflicts between the business interests of the freelancers and the objectivity of their writing.

Many of the irregulars came from smaller countries: Algeria, Belgium, Bosnia, Bulgaria, Colombia, Denmark, Hungary, Ireland, Macedonia, Mauritania, Netherlands, Portugal, Romania, Senegal, Slovakia, Sweden. Some of them were essentially stringers, covering the sort of hard news events that normally would be handled by the traditional foreign correspondents of major newspapers posted in Washington and New York, if their countries had such operations. Irregulars from Bulgaria, Macedonia, and Bosnia were covering a NATO summit on the day that we surveyed them.

The U.S. ethnic press also provides a market for the irregulars. There have been foreign language publications in the United States at least since Benjamin Franklin published a German-language newspaper in Germantown, Pennsylvania, in the 1740s. But the ethnic press has burgeoned in recent years. Margaret Engel reported in 2003 that there were thirty Vietnamese publications in Orange County, California, and that in the San Francisco Bay area there were fourteen media outlets serving the Filipino community alone.[15] One 2004 guide to the ethnic press lists more than 250 publications in New York City, including the *Afghan Communicator,* published in English, Dari, and Pashtu.[16] Among our respondents, Marek Tomaszewski, a correspondent for the Polish Press Agency, freelanced seventy-eight articles for different Polish American newspapers in New York in a year; John O'Mahony, who held dual Irish and U.S. citizenship, worked for the *Irish Independent* (Dublin) and the *Irish Echo* (New York); and Piero Piccardi appeared in *America Oggi* (New York) and *Informazioni per il Commercio Estero* (Milan).[17] Tomasz Deptula's "The Lottery Scams," published in *Nowy Dziennik/Polish Daily News* (New York), exposed "many instances of false information regarding the Green Card Lottery being spread using the Internet."[18] Others listed articles for the ethnic press of Colombia, Hungary, India, and Romania.

Since these correspondents were not sent by their newspapers, magazines, or TV networks to report on the United States, what they wrote about often reflected more idiosyncratic interests:

—Maria Elena Matheus-Atchley, a Venezuelan, was a correspondent for *Tierramerica Environmental Magazine*, which was edited in Mexico and circulated in the Latin American countries. That took a quarter of her time; otherwise, she worked on "short-term communications and PR projects." She had just completed a 2,000-word article on "climate change."[19]

—Max Westerman, who co-owned a small business in New York, did stories for Dutch television. His 210-second short on a high school prom—something that he said that he had wanted to do for a long time—featured a girl, her mother, her boyfriend, her hairdresser, and a "show-off."[20]

—Charles Seife, an American, worked for a British magazine, *New Scientist*. His article, "Dangerous Din," begins, "The international space station will be so noisy that astronauts may struggle to communicate, suffer poor health, and even miss crucial warning tones that signal an emergency. . . ."[21]

—Nicole O'Neill, who had dual American and Swedish citizenship, spent half her time freelancing for various Swedish publications; she also was a language teacher and a waitress. Her "most recent" article was an interview with Marcus Samuelsson, wunderkind chef and co-owner of Aquavit in New York, who was born in Ethiopia, raised by a Swedish family, and trained in Switzerland.[22]

—Theresa Beco do Lobo was a schoolteacher in New York whose articles on the arts scene for two Portuguese magazines, *Moda E Moda* and *Casa E Jardim*, included grandly illustrated accounts of "the great exhibitions" of Jackson Pollock, Mary Cassatt, and John Singer Sargent.[23]

The most moving of the articles that the irregulars sent us was an elegy to America's Memorial Day, by Yve Laudy, published in Belgium's *L'Echo*, June 3, 1999. It begins (in her translation):

"Come into the countryside, Memorial Day isn't fun in New York," Jacques had said last Monday in proposing a barbecue between friends in his distant suburb. For Kevin, equally passionate about the Indianapolis 500 as the Forbes 500, this was a weekend of strong emotions with 350,000 other racing fans. Eve had planned to go to the beach with Jenny and to dig up the best finds in the boutiques on this big day for sales. "That's disgusting," grumbled Ben. "Doesn't anyone remember that on the last Monday in May one honors ex-soldiers?" He's right . . . this has become a holiday more hybrid than patriotic.

Laudy then relates the history of Memorial Day from its proclamation in 1868 before returning to her friends' "microcosm" of Memorial Day: "patriotism, politics, commercialism, and hedonism."[24]

Yve Laudy died at sixty-six years of age on August 28, 2004, at her home in Arlington, Virginia. Her life reflects some of the risk taking and spunkiness that one often finds among the irregulars of the foreign press corps. According to an unsigned obituary in the *Washington Post*,

> In 1971, she sold her advertising agency [in Brussels] and came to the United States to help her mother start a restaurant in Palm Springs, California. The restaurant, specializing in Belgian pastries and other delicacies, didn't work out, so she moved to Los Angeles. Hoping for a career in journalism, she began writing freelance articles. Because she needed a more reliable source of income, she bought a Polaroid camera and took photos of tourists on Hollywood Boulevard. Eventually, she hooked up with a Quebec radio station and began calling in news reports about President Richard Nixon's Western White House, down the coast at San Clemente. That led to a column for a French-language daily newspaper in Quebec. . . .[25]

The publications that the irregulars wrote for spanned the range of their interests: a Japanese newspaper about fashion, an Italian publication about the tobacco industry, a Hungarian magazine about opera, a Chinese journal on medicine, a magazine called *Planet Pop*, and a channel, *TV Cultura*, both in Brazil. There was also a website called the Tocqueville Connection, whose aim was "furthering a dialogue on Franco-American relations."

The output of irregulars may be considerable, but their reach is modest. They rarely appear in the most prestigious international outlets, hence they fall beneath the radar of opinionmakers. They may have an impact through specialized publications, but it would be hard to measure. Overwhelmingly, they appear to have come to the United States from somewhere else and to intend to stay (see figure 2, page 49). That distinguishes them from freelancers who work abroad

FIGURE 2. Citizenship of Irregular Foreign Correspondents[a]

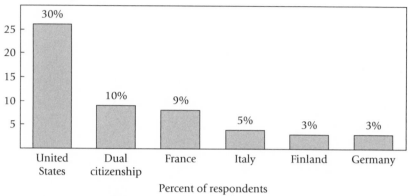

Number of respondents

Percent of respondents

a. Number of respondents = 87.

for American news organizations in the hope that eventually they will find a job as a traditional foreign correspondent or some other permanent assignment.[26] The irregulars in America are much less likely to be journalists-in-training and much more likely to be amateurs or hobbyists. They lean toward soft news in a hard news world: an Argentine, for example, writing about the weather in New York during a period of extreme cold in Buenos Aires[27] or an Australian writing about Manhattan's East Village, "wandering about the neighborhood, talking to people, my own memories and experiences."[28] There are some ideologues in the mix, but the group's interests are generally less political than those of the traditional correspondents who are sent to Washington to cover government. Indeed, a disproportionate number of the irregulars live in places other than Washington. Also, perhaps because they are less likely to be writing about public policy, perhaps because they are not as controlled by editors overseas, perhaps because they have made their home in the United States, their stories appear to present a kinder, gentler portrait of America and Americans.[29]

Hollywood

A subject the world loves

"I srael has an insatiable appetite for Hollywood stories," said Tom Tugend, a Los Angeles stringer for the *Jerusalem Post*, when we interviewed him in 1999. So, apparently, do Brazil, Australia, and Senegal. Danielle Machado Duran, a freelancer in New York, reported that a Brazilian magazine had just requested an article on the movie *The Blair Witch Project*. Mark Riley, of the *Sydney Morning Herald*, had just returned to New York from Los Angeles, where he was covering the Academy Awards. Aly K. Ndaw was doing an article, "Black Americans in the Cinema," for a Senegalese newspaper. "I love movies," he told us.

How the foreign media cover the American entertainment industry—its products and its personalities—is a controversial matter. *Suddeutsche Zeitung,* one of Germany's most respected newspapers, confessed in 2000 that some of its Hollywood stories were fabricated in Los Angeles by Tom Kummer, a Swiss journalist, who also wrote for a number of leading German magazines. His articles were filled with ersatz confidences from the stars—Whitney Houston, Brad Pitt, Sharon Stone, Kim Basinger. Kummer's inventions included this quote, attributed to Courtney Love: "I play with my breasts, not to show off but to demonstrate a kind of revulsion. I simply transform myself into a voice for all the tormented souls of this world." And this, ascribed to Ivana Trump: "Pimples are not really a problem. They come and they go. Skin irritations are much worse. It can only get worse when you're turned down by a famous skin clinic." The moral of Kummer's downfall, according to the foreign press corps in Hollywood, is that editors should know that movie industry publicists never give foreigners that kind of access.

"The problem," said Claus Lutterback, who had been a Hollywood correspondent for *Stern* magazine, "is that no one, not even our bosses, knows how Hollywood really works. They don't know how hard it is to get any access at all. They think we spend our time at cocktail parties with movie stars. So someone like Kummer can come along and they have no control over him."[1]

It was to try to gain access that eight foreigners banded together in 1943 to form the Hollywood Foreign Correspondents Association, renamed the Hollywood Foreign Press Association (HFPA) in 1955. Their brilliant solution to "the cold-shoulder treatment they routinely received from the studios," according to Louis B. Hobson of the *Calgary Sun*, was that "instead of writing a host of negative stories, the eight wisely chose to honour the very people who were snubbing them."[2] Or, in the words of the HFPA's publicity department, "The group's members felt it was incumbent upon them to give their audience their judgments as to Hollywood's finest productions."[3] The first award for best picture was presented in 1944 to *The Song of Bernadette*. The next year the trophies were named the Golden Globes.

The group's by-laws cap membership at one hundred; there were ninety-four members in 2004.[4] The small number of members, regardless of the quality of their output, has often been criticized—so much power to so few—especially as the Golden Globes have gained importance as a marketing tool in the movie industry. The Academy of Motion Picture Arts and Sciences, which awards the Oscars, has a membership in the 6,000 range. But HFPA was designed to provide access to movie stars and directors, and that access is offered to members only at press conferences now held in the organization's West Hollywood clubhouse. And access, of course, is about keeping out as well as letting in. As Helmut Voss, of Germany's Springer Publications and a former HFPA president, put it: "We have a certain protection system in place that safeguards against conflict. If a freelancer claimed to work for one of the newspapers in my group, I would examine those credentials very carefully."[5] "Any single member can blackball an applicant," writes Sharon Waxman, who has covered Hollywood for the *Washington Post* and the *New York Times* and who views the HFPA with a critical eye.[6] Lorenzo Soria, of Italy's *La Stampa* and HFPA president in 2004, told Waxman,

> Personally, I would like to see the number of our members increase. I'm also aware that there is a limit to how much we

can increase, because the main perk we have are press conferences. You cannot have a press conference with 200 journalists. Some of our members have a hard time making a
living as journalists. There are competition issues.[7]

Theo Kingma, a photographer for *Dutch*, a fashion and lifestyle magazine, attended 200 HFPA press conferences in 1998; Norwegian freelancer Aud Berggren told the *Hollywood Reporter*, "I would not have
survived without the HFPA."[8]

The Golden Globe awards have a sullied history, mostly relating to
gifts and press junkets. In 1999, for instance, Sharon Stone, a Golden
Globe nominee, sent each HFPA member a luxury Coach watch, valued between $300 and $400. "This watch was way, way, way beyond
the edge of the envelope as far as promotional considerations, like
T-shirts," responded then President Voss, who made his members
return the gift. (They were allowed, however, to keep $35 cell phones).[9]

One scandal may taint the HFPA forever: in 1982, the ultra-rich
husband of actress Pia Zadora bankrolled a "field trip" to Las Vegas for
members, and the group later awarded Zadora a Golden Globe for her
performance in a soft-core adult film. CBS dropped the awards show,
and it did not reappear on network TV until it was reinstated by NBC
in 1996. NBC made the HFPA clean up its act. Movie stars could no
longer sign autographs for members at their press conferences or give
special receptions and live performances in honor of the group. Nor
could members' promotional gifts be grander than those given to
other journalists.[10]

For its money, NBC got "one of the most important and powerful
events on the Hollywood calendar . . . [p]artly because its reputation
as a raucous party has made it a magnet for celebrities. But mostly, it
is because the television ratings for the awards ceremony have steadily
increased."[11] It is now the third-most-watched awards telecast, after the
Oscars and the Grammys, having at times reached an audience of more
than 23 million. In recent years, the *New York Times* has devoted forty
inches of column space to both the nominations and the winners. In
2004 it ran an article with a four-column photograph on what female
members of the HFPA would be wearing at the awards ceremony.[12]

NBC pays the organization $2.5 million a year, which may make
HFPA the richest press association in the world. The agreement expires
in 2011. With NBC's money, HFPA allows its members to take two fully
paid trips a year to film festivals of their choice anywhere in the world

and pays air fare for studio press junkets.[13] HFPA also contributes to film-related charities; it gave more than $600,000 in 2003.

As the Golden Globes have become increasingly prominent in the entertainment industry, with foreign box office revenues from American movies growing faster than domestic, the characterization of HFPA members in the American press has taken on an increasingly sharp edge. They have been called "a small, slightly louche clique of Hollywood hangers-on" by Alessandra Stanley, *New York Times;* a "group of eccentric Hollywood parasites," by Adam Buckman, *New York Post;* and "bottom-feeders" by John Powers, film critic for *LA Weekly,* appearing on a television documentary, "Golden Globes: Hollywood's Dirty Little Secret."[14] "They're like the Beverly Hillbillies," said a Hollywood publicist. "They're not sophisticated."[15]

Peter Bart of *Variety* finds this "tone of righteous indignation to be a little tiring."[16] But it is intriguing. Who are these people, who give their awards to just about the same movies as then win Oscars? Are they slightly louche—a slightly archaic way of calling them disreputable?

In 1999 we interviewed nineteen of the eighty-two then-active members of the HFPA and subsequently searched for others through the Internet. Among our findings were Vera Anderson, photographer and author of *A Woman Like You,* a remarkable study of domestic violence; Armando Gallo, author of books whose photographs trace the careers of Peter Gabriel and the British rock band Genesis; Avik Gilboa, photojournalist and president of the Gustav Mahler Society in America; Mike Goodridge, author of *Screencraft: Directing,* a collection of interviews with fifteen important directors, supplemented with storyboards, script excerpts, and notebooks from their work; Emanuel Levy, a student of sociologist Robert K. Merton and an author who saw his books on Hollywood as part of "a coherent research agenda"; Lisa Lu, an actress best known for her roles in *The Last Emperor* and *The Joy Luck Club;* Howard Lucraft, a composer, arranger, and guitarist whose Hollywood reports appeared in *Crescendo and Jazz Music* (United Kingdom); Mira Vukelich Panajotovic, once an international tennis player, now recognized for devising effective ways to teach English; Patrick Roth, prize-winning author of complex German novels; Marianne Ruuth, author of *Skin Deep* (described as a book about "those who grow up half-black, half-white, who walk the line between two cultures, two colors"), founder of a newsletter "concerning African-Americans in the film industry," and translator of Ingmar Bergman's

My Life in Film; and Aida Takia O'Reilly, professor of Pan-African Studies, California State University, Los Angeles.

When asked the same question—"Who are the members of the HFPA?"—Sharon Waxman answers:

> Perhaps two dozen are working foreign journalists; a larger number are long-time members who freelance infrequently for small overseas publications. Many are Americans, many live on their pensions—three are now in their nineties, many others in their eighties—and struggle to produce the four yearly clippings they need to qualify as active members. A large number of HFPA members make their living at other professions, including teaching, real estate, car sales and film promotion.

Waxman is not wrong in characterizing the members as she does, merely selective, as is our list in the previous paragraph.

A more typical profile of an HFPA member might be that of Saverio Lomedico, who died in 1999, in his early eighties. He reported for various Italian newspapers and magazines, but he also had small parts in several movies, served as Federico Fellini's interpreter in America and John Ford's interpreter in Italy, and was a technical adviser for television shows in need of Italian authenticity.[17]

HFPA members' work fits unevenly into three categories of movie journalism. There are a few—but very few—who are the equivalent of Waxman, reporters for mainstream news organizations assigned to cover Hollywood as an industry. That is the major complaint about the group's composition. (Most critical articles will note that a *Le Monde* correspondent has been repeatedly rejected for membership.)[18] There also are a few—but very few—who write about the art of cinema (this is not an organization of film critics). Basically, HFPA members practice celebrity journalism.

"Nicole Kidman is the epitome of class," begins an article by Aniko Navi in *Solitaire* (Singapore), December–January 2002–03. "As the first October morning buries the Los Angeles sky in a grey blanket, she defiantly lights up the room with a magic touch of everlasting spring. . . ." And Noel De Souza opens his article for *Mid Day* (India), October 11, 2003: "How could I not accept an invitation from Warner Brothers Studios to visit the sets of the [Harry Potter] film in London. For me it would be a reunion with an old friend, director Alfonso Cuaron. . . ."

Much celebrity journalism is in the form of question-and-answer pieces. Colin Firth, interviewed by Gabrielle Donnelly, *Real Magazine* (United Kingdom), August 13–26, 2002, had this to say:

Q. *Be honest now—what do you think about the name Colin?*

A. Well, it doesn't exactly have a ring to it, does it? It's more the sort of name you'd give your goldfish for a joke.

And Russell Crowe, interviewed by Edmund Brettschneider, *TV Movie* (Germany), February 15, 2002, revealed his technique for choosing roles (in translation):

Q: *How do you select your roles?*

A: I blindfold my eyes and throw a [expletive] dart.

Q: *And in reality?*

A: When I get goose bumps reading a script, I'll do the film.

A website that catalogues publicity about Tom Hanks lists interviews, articles, or cover photographs of the actor in nine U.K. outlets (*Blast, Empire, Evening Standard Hot Tickets, Filmlink, Film Review, Flicks, Premiere, Radio Time, Sight and Sound*) and six in Germany (*Cinema, Gong, Spielfilm, TV Movie, TV-Spielfilm, Widescreen*). The website for Charlize Theron lists similar articles from Australia, Canada, Denmark, Germany, Hungary, Italy, Japan, Portugal, South Africa, Sweden, and the United Kingdom. And we turned up the following for fans of Keanu Reeves: "Keanu Reeves, con una nueva chica en Australia," *Semana* (Spain), January 9, 2002; "Heimatloser Rocker," *In Style* (Germany), June 2002; "Tempo fuori luogo," *Film TV* (Italy), July 2002; "Keanu Reeves: 'J'ai vraiment arrete mes conneries, je ne suis plus le nombril du monde," *Entrevue* (France), July 2002; and "Why Keanu Won't Play Ball," *Scotsman* (United Kingdom), June 16, 2002.

The insatiable appetite for Hollywood stories is reflected in publications throughout the world that make a profit from celebrity journalism. Is this foreign correspondence? Big time. It's journalism that follows a simple rule, outlined by longtime HFPA member Anita Weber: "I like to describe what the star is doing, their latest movie and whether it was good or bad. If it's good, I will say so. If it's bad, I just forget about it, because I'm not going to bite the hand that feeds me."[19]

In America

It's not like being in any other country

"Ithink one of the extraordinary things about being here is periodically getting these feelings of déjà vu as you see streetscapes or squares, and you suddenly think, 'I've been here before,' and you realize that it was in a movie," said Patrick Smyth, Washington correspondent for the *Irish Times*.[1] "Growing up in South Africa, coming here," said Pierre Steyn, also in Washington, "it was like there was nothing strange about this place, 'cause you can see it on television."[2]

No one comes to the United States without preconceptions. Of course, many respondents to our survey had already spent time in America before returning as foreign correspondents. A third of the non-Americans had studied in the United States, some as high school exchange students, several even as pupils in elementary school.[3] (See figure 1, page 57.) "I lived here and went to school here from when I was seven 'til I was twelve," said the *Economist*'s John Parker.[4] "I was thirteen years old when my parents sent me to this country to study and learn English," said Jacobo Goldstein from Honduras.[5] "I didn't come here the first time as a correspondent," said Tom Buhrow, Washington bureau chief of ARD, German Television. "I went to high school for two years in Wisconsin. You know [after I attended high school in America], some of my deepest friendships are with Americans."[6] Shinichiro Sakikawa, of *Hokkaidu Shimbun*, went to high school in Washington and then spent his first university year at MIT.[7] Masao Hosoda, Kyodo News Service, was an exchange student for a year at the University of Missouri, Columbia.[8] B. J. Yang, *Korea Economic Daily*, earned a Ph.D. in finance at

FIGURE 1. Correspondents Who Studied in the United States[a]

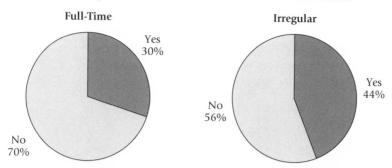

a. Number of respondents: full-time = 287; irregular = 55. Respondents who were American citizens were excluded.

the University of Kansas.[9] Sridhar Krishnaswami, the *Hindu*, earned his Ph.D. in political science from Miami University, in Ohio.[10]

One of the distinguishing characteristics of correspondents who work around the world for American news organizations is that they too have spent extended periods of their youth abroad.[11] Becoming a foreign correspondent is part of a self-selection process. "I fought my way to this place," said Adnan Aljadi, of the Kuwait News Agency in Washington.[12] These are people who are open to the experience of mixing with people of other cultures.

Yet our foreign correspondents arrived in the United States with a collection of stereotypes that they said were cherished by the people in their countries. When they described those images of America, nearly half (49 percent) of them fit in the *superpower* category: "hegemonic," "imperialistic," "haughty," "arrogant," "selfish." There were some countries, however, such as Taiwan, where calling the United States "the world's policeman" was not a slur. *Western hero*, the next-largest category, was mentioned by 24 percent of respondents; it included such characterizations as "individualistic," "competitive," "materialistic," "brash," and "aggressive." Seventeen percent of the correspondents mentioned variations on *provincial*: "lacking knowledge of the rest of the world," "uneducated," "ignorant," "naïve." Twelve percent described the *ugly American*—fat, loud, and rude—while 11 percent said that Americans were viewed as *flag-wavers* who stressed patriotism, freedom, and democracy. "The land of golden opportunity" was the stereotype of America in Poland, according to Pawel Burdzy.[13]

Many of the impressions were sharpened by disagreements with various U.S. government policies.[14] *To Vima* correspondent Dimitris Apokis spoke of the "animosity from the Greek military junta in 1974" as well as "the Cyprus issue."[15] "As you know," said Dubravka Savic, *Belgrade Daily,* "Yugoslavia was attacked by NATO in 1999, and it was seen as an American intervention."[16] In the words of Mohammed Said, of Egypt's *Al-Ahram:*

> In the case of a Palestinian who sees his people so brutally victimized by the Israelis, who are totally unleashed by the Americans—there is no doubt about it, systematically destroyed—that normally a person with good sense [will not change his opinion]. It's like, if you hate me that much, then why [should I like you?]"[17]

(Our survey was conducted before the Iraq war and does not reflect the anti-American sentiment that it unleashed. However, the interviews that we conducted after the invasion of Afghanistan did not reflect changes in correspondents' attitudes.)

The correspondents told us, as expected, that stereotypes did not affect their stories. Almost invariably they added something like "I need to recognize stereotypes in order to work against them." Yet several brave correspondents chose not to give such socially acceptable responses. Chang Choi of Korea TV explained,

> Our upper-middle class is pro-American. From the middle class and below, they hearken to [a negative image]. From the point of a news organization, a much greater chunk of our audience is from the middle class. So we cannot [ignore] this majority. Our editors put weight on this anti-United States sentiment. Some stories [that are] negative to the United States are appealing to these classes.[18]

Olivier Knox of Agence France-Presse noted, "We pay a lot of attention to death penalty stuff; that's a topic we cover because it gets big play in France. There is necessarily an element, and I think it's a very small element, of being a foreign correspondent that involves reinforcing the home country's prejudices."[19] For Lauren Chambliss, reporting from Washington for the *Evening Standard* (London), stereotypical descriptors included "crass," "driven," and "uncultured." "I do stories that reinforce the stereotypes," she said.[20] Freelance German radio correspondent Annette Moll, when asked about stereotypes, replied, "Oh, Americans! Obesity . . . fast food chains. . . . Great topic! That's very American. So from the point of view of me being also a businesswoman, because I have to sell my stories, I would say that's a good topic to write about."[21]

The United States is not a hardship post. The water is clean. The transportation system is good. The natives are friendly. The scenery is sometimes spectacular. Judging the relative cost of goods and services depends on where you're coming from. And the work differs markedly from what increasingly is being reported from the rest of the world, where, as media scholar Philip Seib notes, "war continues to be a growth industry."[22]

Moreover, most of the correspondents are headquartered in New York or Washington, which are considered comfort zones. "It's a very easy place to live," said Julian Borger, a *Guardian* correspondent in Washington:

> It's very cosmopolitan. It's not like living in Topeka or a place where people are used to fewer accents and they are occasions for comment, as it would be elsewhere. A good example is the World Cup. People are in bars [watching the games at night], people actually know what you're talking about here, whereas they're not [watching or talking about it] in Peoria, or wherever. You really feel that you're at least on a coast and the foreign influence sort of wafts in with the wind.[23]

Jorge Banales, a Uruguayan who reports for EFE News Service (Spain), agreed. "I love Washington. . . . You can visit restaurants or see theater or get in touch with people from all over the world." But he acknowledged that there was something that he missed:

> I miss radio. I love radio. In other countries you have radio [stations] that play all kinds of music. Because our education is more multicultural—we learn French, for example, and Portuguese—you can in Uruguay listen to music from France and Brazil. Here . . . the country music station is only country music. Jazz station is only jazz all day. And you cannot ever hear music from other parts of the world on the radio. That part I miss.[24]

Yasemin Congar, Washington bureau chief of *Milliyet*, recalled working in Europe: "In London, you would always feel you are a Turk. . . .
In Brussels, you would always feel you are a Turk." But in Washington
and New York, she continued, "You're not as interesting or as exotic.
You don't stand out as much, which is good."[25]

The correspondents with school-age children were generally satis-
fied with their children's schooling and pleased that the children were
bilingual. Most expressed the importance of instilling a sense of native
culture in their children, yet acknowledged that the process of Americanization was inevitable. Explained Charles Groenhuijsen, of NOS,
Dutch radio and TV:[26]

> **Groenhuijsen:** I would say that the kids are Dutch American.
> They wake up in English. I wake up in Dutch. They go to reg-
> ular public elementary school in Bethesda [Maryland]. . . .
> They sing "Proud to be an American." They come home
> and say, "George Washington was our first president." [But]
> they still consider themselves to be Dutch.
>
> **Q:** *Do you speak Dutch at home?*
>
> **A:** As much as possible. But it's getting tough. Among them-
> selves they tend to speak English.
>
> **Q:** *Is their Dutch passable?*
>
> **A:** Oh, yeah. They tell me, "Daddy, you have such a funny
> accent." I say, "You guys are the ones with the funny accents."
> . . . It's going to be hard for them when we go back eventually
> and they have no clue about geography, no clue about Dutch
> history, European history. This happens to so many kids. But
> all three of them are smart kids. They'll pick it up. I've seen
> so many people go back with kids and say, "Oh, my god, is
> this going to work out in school?" And eventually they come
> back and blend in easily.

"It's a great city for a family," said Christophe de Roquefeuil, who
covered the State Department for Agence France-Presse in 2002. "We
have a nice split-level house with a big yard, something I could not
even dream of in Tehran [his previous post]." There was a problem,

however: his wife, a medical doctor, could not work as a doctor in the United States.[27]

Patrick Smyth called that "the trailing spouses phenomenon"; it also pertains in the case of diplomats and others whose work requires them to move around the world. "You tell your wife, 'I'm sorry, dear, we're moving to X country. You can give up your job and follow me.' And she becomes a trailing spouse." In Smyth's case, he said, "[My wife] was in Brussels for seven years, unable to work. She was here for nine months, unable to work, and has gone back, and is working in Dublin. [She is a lawyer.] So I've been here on my own. But we see each other every three months, which is a bit rough."

Nobu Sakajiri of *Asahi Shimbun* (Japan) told us of the complication in his family:

Q: *Do you have family here? Do you have children?*

A: Yes. They are coming over. One five-year-old. He's very cute. Look at this [*he shows a photograph*].

Q: *What's his name?*

A: Tomo. This is my family [*he gestures to picture*]. They are coming. But my wife has a job which she originally [didn't want] to quit. But I want to be with them, so I persuaded my wife to quit. I feel very sorry, but. . . .

Q: *Is she going to find work here?*

A: No, I don't think so because, same as me, she has a language program, so it's very difficult to [have a] job [on top of that].[28]

We heard other variations of the trailing spouse phenomenon from Russian, Swedish, Slovak, and Kuwaiti correspondents.

An aspect of the correspondent's job in America that can be considered family-friendly was noted by Tim Lester, Australian Broadcasting, when he talked about a previous posting. "When I was in Southwest Asia, I spent 70 percent of my time away. We were based in Bangkok there, which is a great place to be flying to Cambodia and Malaysia and Indonesia."[29] David Shipler, then with the *New York Times*, said he turned down his paper's Kenya bureau because the beat would have included most of Africa, which would have meant being continually away from his family.[30] But two-thirds of our correspondents in the United States said that they were away from home less than thirty-one days a year. Only 15 percent were on the road for more than two months a year.[31]

Although they did not appear to be spending more days away than they had when they were surveyed in 1979, how they spent their time was quite different. The 1979 respondents went to a limited number of states, mostly on the East or West Coast, and only to the big cities. Twenty years later, all regions of the country were well represented: 69 percent of the correspondents had been in the South; 65 percent in the Northeast; 57 percent in the West; and 39 percent in the Midwest. The cities visited by at least 10 percent of the correspondents were New York (50 percent), Los Angeles (28 percent), Washington (28 percent), Chicago (24 percent), Boston (24 percent), San Francisco (20 percent), Miami (18 percent), Denver (14 percent), Houston (12 percent), and Atlanta (10 percent). The next-most-visited cities were Orlando, Las Vegas, San Diego, New Orleans, Seattle, Philadelphia, Detroit, Dallas, Phoenix, and Salt Lake City, which may suggest that some correspondents found ways to vacation and work during the same trip. The big change, however, was that more than one-third of the full-time correspondents—36 percent—listed trips to small cities. The respondents had been to a total of 248 cities in 1998, and many were off the beaten track: Marfa, Texas, population 2,424, county seat of Presidio County, at the junction of U.S. highways 90 and 67; Talladega, Alabama, population 15,026; Warrensburg, Missouri, population 16,938; Kissimmee, Florida, population 41,248, on the northern bank of Lake Tohopekaliga; and Leech Lake, Minnesota, at the heart of the Chippewa National Forest. (See figure 2, page 63, for the number of cities visited by correspondents in 1998.)

Perhaps it was the availability of faster and cheaper air transportation—and for television people the ability to travel lighter—but the correspondents seemed more likely to seek the occasional story away from Washington and New York, especially if they could find a local angle. Lee Siew Hua, the *Straits Times* (Singapore), took a "trip to South Carolina, to Charleston," to do a story "about how they shifted the priorities of the economy once the military bases closed down. And there was some parallel to Singapore, to when the British pulled their bases out and we thought we would collapse."[32] For Tim Lester, the story was about "some firefighters from Australia and New Zealand [who] are coming up to help with the Western [forest] fire. It's inter-

FIGURE 2. Number of U.S. Cities Visited by Correspondents in 1998[a]

Percent of respondents

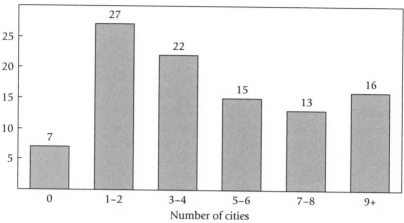

Number of cities

a. Number of respondents = 387.

esting." Patrick Smyth reported, "I had a wonderful trip to Alaska last year—ANWR [Arctic National Wildlife Refuge], 200 miles north of the Arctic Circle in mid-February, and it was a real boys-zone adventure. It was lovely." Lars Moberg, of Swedish Television, noted that "if you get an idea, you can be at National Airport in an hour and you can go to wherever and you can travel around. That's good."[33] Still, it all came down to the bottom line: "I travel very rarely," said Tomasz Zalewski, in Washington for the Polish Press Agency. "Our agency doesn't have the money for that. I will sometimes go to New York. I will sometimes go to Chicago. But very rarely, for lack of resources."[34]

"I am old enough to come [here] with stereotypes that [Americans] are fat, stupid, that they eat hamburgers and whatever," said Olga Bakova of Slovakia's Radio Slovensko. "But you have delicious restaurants, nice people. I have never met angry people who push me aside. Whenever I ask something, [Americans] are always willing to answer me. And if they have no answer, they direct me somewhere [where I can get the information]."[35] What may confound an American is how much the correspondents kept stressing the niceness of Americans. "I have been surprised by how friendly people are here," said Ibru Wane of Senegal. "I didn't expect to be accepted so easily. This is a country of immigration. I think everyone here has been an immigrant in one way."[36] "People are extremely nice [here]. I mean it," said Charles Groenhuijsen, the Dutch TV correspondent.

There were critics. Jesus Esquivel of Notimex, the Mexican news service, told us, "It is very difficult to accommodate yourself in this country [to the American way of life]. I cannot say culture, because obviously there is no culture in this country, there is no history. And it's not an offense, but it's true, you don't even know your neighbor."[37] The few other personal (as distinct from professional) complaints about Americans came from post-9/11 indignities, often relating to airport searches. "They do random checks before boarding, and always I am picked for random checks," said Takeshi Yamashita of NHK-TV. "Maybe they [think] I am North Korean. I'd like to say Japan is a key ally to the United States . . . so I don't [deserve] to be discriminated [against] in the United States."[38] A very upset Arab journalist told us, "I don't want to go into specifics, but she almost reached into my crotch."[39] Yet despite what they considered harsh airport experiences, Arab correspondents also offered some of the most enthusiastic assessments of America. An Egyptian, after recounting "a whole number of threats [from callers to] our telephone line in our office," added, "otherwise, my deepest conviction is that the American society is essentially a good society in a way that you rarely see elsewhere. . . . My essential image of Americans is extremely positive."[40]

Do correspondents become more pro-American the longer they stay in America? "I think that's inevitable," said Karin Henriksson of Svenska Dagbladet.[41] Mike Hayashi of Yomiuri Shimbun agreed: "Over time, if [Japanese correspondents] had prejudices, as they stay in America our people see how friendly America is. They understand more. . . . The longer you're here, you become part of it. And there's a saying that if you lived in one place [for a long time], it becomes your capital."[42]

We asked our correspondents whether their editors ever asked for stories that might reinforce stereotypes, like the image of fat Americans and fast food. Yasemin Congar replied: "Yes, quite a bit. It's very challenging [because] editors ask for such a story, and you would say, 'This is not the way you think it is. It is or this is not that bad.' And they would say, 'Oh, she is just so pro-American now.' " Julian Borger observed that "the more you're here, the more you tend to resist the demand to feed this stereotype of middle America."

Michel Faure, who had been the Washington correspondent of Liberation, "a French newspaper with leftist tendencies," during Ronald

Reagan's presidency, later recalled that while some of his French colleagues "regularly reminded their readers that the U.S. president had at one point been associated with a chimpanzee named Bonzo," he "found it hard not to like Reagan." "Under Reagan," he said, "I came to understand the strength of America's founding values [which] made it such an exceptional nation, the 'city on the hill.' "[43]

We asked our correspondents how the stories that their home office wanted differed from those that they initiated. "They are interested in stories that have a greater content in Greek subjects," replied Panagiotis Papadopoulos.[44] The same response—that the correspondents were losing sight of whom they were reporting for—was heard from correspondents from Australia, Brazil, Canada, Denmark, Finland, France, Germany, Great Britain, Holland, Israel, Italy, Japan, Mexico, Nigeria, Spain, and Sweden. All foreign editors rightly worry about their faraway correspondents "going native." In America the problem is especially acute, as the process of "Americanization" often creates conflicts with their nation's stereotypes of America.

How
They Work

"Being a foreign correspondent is great; I love it. No bureaucracy. You call people [in other jobs] and they tell you, 'Oh, I'm in a meeting.' Me, I'm never in a meeting. Yeah, every now and then a couple of minutes, but usually I'm at work doing stuff."

—Charles Groenhuijsen, NOS, *Dutch radio and TV*,
July 7, 2002

"The British press is much more stretched than the American. You don't even realize the comparison; the work rate is much higher. You tend to produce many more items in less time."

—Julian Borger, *Guardian* (United Kingdom),
June 14, 2002

"Increasingly in the world's point of view, the story in America seems to be in Washington. Washington sucks us in so much and so much centers on Washington. In fact, my boss is forever complaining we don't see enough of middle America. We don't see enough of Boise, Idaho, or Albuquerque. But on a day-to-day level, they're saying You're right. I like the Boise, Idaho, idea. It's great. But today, give me Iraq."

—Tim Lester, Australian Broadcasting Corporation,
August 8, 2002

"I do some, you know, Swedish things that would be of interest to Swedish readers. In New York I met two people that are actively involved in promoting Swedish exports. I put something together, and we had a sort of roundtable discussion, just taping what they're saying and then transcribing it. But it's still something more [than] just the news."

—Karin Henriksson, *Svenska Dagbladet*,
June 26, 2002

"A lot of days what I do is sort of a natural construction of what happened yesterday. Israel bombs Gaza, a U.S. reaction story, how this is going to affect the U.S. peace efforts."

—Janine Zacharia, *Jerusalem Post*,
July 25, 2002

"It is another difficult thing [because] if you go [to briefings], you go for a whole day and do nothing [else]. I am the only one, so I have to be very rational about my time. Even my phone calls, not to think of going out. I have only one day, and with the time difference. . . ."

—Dubravka Savic, *Belgrade Daily*,
August 7, 2002

"Well, you don't always see eye to eye [with your editors] on questions concerning the U.S. The perception is different. If you are in Italy, you tend to look at the U.S. in a very tainted way. If you are here, you have the knowledge they don't have. So sometimes you have to push to convince them the meaning of the story is this."

—Ennino Carreto, *Corriere Della Sera* (Italy),
June 5, 2002

"There [are] always discrepancies between the correspondents and the head desk, and you try and work out these differences. But I'm a believer that the desk is the final judge. Whatever they say, if you cannot convince them, if they insist, you have to go by that. You have to do whatever they want. Because I worked on the main desk, I know how it feels to be there, it's a frustrating job, you keep waiting for stories."

—Adnan Aljadi, Kuwait News Agency,
August 14, 2002

Time

Adjusting to deadlines around the world

What distinguishes most foreign correspondents from most other journalists is that often they are separated from their editors and audience by several time zones. Those who work in New York or Washington usually are six hours behind Europe and twelve to fourteen hours ahead of Asia. "The time difference is the hardest part," Dubravka Savic of *Belgrade Daily* told us. "I'm always running after time and never reaching it."[1]

The most obvious consequence of reporting on breaking news for a distant organization is that the workday becomes very long. "I love to work in this country," said Rujun Wang, of China's *People's Daily*. "But you have to work very hard, especially [since] we have a time difference. You have to work too hard, I think. Sometimes I realize I have to work harder than American people, but I don't make more money than they do."[2] "I am practically overrun by the amount of work I have to do," concluded Ennino Carreto of Italy's *Corriere Della Sera*.[3]

Correspondents can run into problems trying to fit events that transpire in one place to deadlines designed for somewhere else. "We don't pay attention to most State Department briefings," commented Julian Borger of the *Guardian*. "It's late for us, timing-wise. Five hours' difference."[4] But mid-morning briefings were fine for Toshiyuki Matsuyama, of Fuji TV; adjusting to what happens at night was his problem: "President Bush made a speech for the public, for [the] TV camera. That happens always at night, eastern time. In that case, we have to do a live report from here soon after we hear the speech."[5] Japanese papers want the big stories for the morning news. At *Yomiuri Shimbun*'s Washington bureau, according to Mike Hayashi, "We have an annex room where we can sleep."[6]

Juggling time zones has consequences for correspondents' personal lives. "I can't see my kid," said Chang Choi of Korea TV. "I get up late, after 9:00, 10:00, and my kid already went to school."[7]

The time factor is illustrated in the following accounts of "typical" days from some foreign correspondents in Washington. The first are from those who report to Europe: Olga Bakova, Yasemin Congar, Lars Moberg, and Patrick Smyth. Morning deadlines morph into evening deadlines for the correspondents who report to Asia: Takeshi Yamashita, Chang Choi, and Nobu Sakajiri.

Olga Bakova, Radio Slovensko, Slovakia (July 11, 2002)

Bakova: Generally in the morning, like 9 o'clock in the morning, which is 3:00 p.m. over there, [my editors] call me and ask me what is going on. And I wake up [before that], I go through my newspapers, usually *Washington Post, Washington Times, New York Times*, sometimes Internet. And my apartment and my office is the same, so it's very easy. I try to go to the AP and all kinds of websites, other agencies, of course TV. And I tell [my editors] that this and this and this happened. And I have to ask them what do they want. What's going on [here] doesn't mean it is interesting in Europe. There are some cases, like the little girl from Utah [Elizabeth Smart], nobody cares about it in Slovakia. I don't want to feed them with it.

We also have late evening programs. But usually they just repeat [what I reported] at 6:00 in the evening. Usually I do a news story, then I am working on different kinds of [feature stories during the other half of the day]. For example, I was in New York, and I went all [over] Brooklyn. I went many different kinds of places, so I brought my [materials back to Washington] and I have to make different things for different kinds of programs. I interviewed one woman from Afghanistan, so I had to prepare these materials. Usually I work all day, then in the evening, 5, 6 o'clock, I start work for my morning and mid-day programs [back home]. And I do it through Internet. My only contact [with my editors] is by telephone in the morning, because it is easier and cheaper to mix all these radio things and send it.

Q: *You send them the finished product?*

A: Yes. Through FTP [file transfer protocol] transmission.

Q: *You have this technology in your apartment?*

A: Yes, I have everything. I [cut and edit the pieces], and I have different kinds of programs for mixing. So if Colin Powell says something, I have to translate it, but also to mix it together.

Q: *So you're the writer, the editor, the translator, and the producer?*

A: Everything. Driver and mother of two kids.

Q: *That must keep you very busy.*

A: Of course. But it depends how you look at it. This is a very interesting job. Sometimes I work until 2 o'clock in the morning. That's when they have morning news [in Slovakia]. And when it's important, I do live shows. And I don't care, because I like it.

Yasemin Congar, *Milliyet* and CNN Turk, Turkey (July 19, 2002)

Congar: The newspaper I work for is part of the biggest media group in Turkey. I work for the newspaper [*Milliyet*] as the Washington bureau chief, as the foreign affairs columnist. I also work for CNN Turk, which is a news network. So I work for two different organizations within the same umbrella. [CNN Turk] is a twenty-four-hour news network just like CNN. It's owned by Turner International and our media corporation. They call me at 1:00 a.m. [Washington time], and I do the 6:00 or 7:00 a.m [news in Turkey]. Between 1:00 a.m. and 2:00 a.m. [in Washington], which is the prime-time news [in Turkey], that's my political portion, sometimes live, sometimes recorded. For the newspaper I usually talk to them around 6:30 [a.m. in Washington] or so and we decide if I'm doing a story. Or if I have a story already, we decide how I'm going to use it. Then I have an early deadline for the early edition at 9:00 [a.m. in Washington]. And for the late edition, it ends up usually 2:00 p.m. [in Washington]. It can go as late as 6:00 p.m. for an important story.

I write columns. I have two weekly columns. One is a political column, one is a cultural column. One is in the Sunday edition, the cultural column, and the other appears on Monday on the foreign news page. And I write them the last day, especially the political column. The political column I have to file it by 9:00 a.m. Then I usually get up by 5:00 a.m. to do it. But I have done all the interviews and I have all the notes. I [just] get up and write it.

Basically you work on tomorrow's story today, in the afternoon. But TV changes that because we can record anything anytime. It's a twenty-four-hour news network. And it's immediate. If I have an important story and it's exclusive, I usually break it on TV whenever it happened, whenever I learn about [it]. And when I write something on that for the paper [after I've already broken it on TV], they don't like that. But because both organizations are owned by the same company, they're not competitive in that sense directly, and they have an understanding. Only when the newspaper asks me about something exclusively—if they say, "I want an exclusive interview on this"—then I wouldn't do anything [on the same subject for TV].

Lars Moberg, Swedish Television (June 13, 2002)

Moberg: I come in at 8:30 or 9:00 in the morning, and I get down to my desk. Then, of course, I have already in my house been on the computer the first thing when I wake up just to check the mail. With the time difference e-mail is even more essential. You have six hours. They're six hours ahead of us here. So when I wake up in the United States the day has almost passed in Sweden.

I have two main programs that I work for. One of them is 7:30 p.m. in Sweden, which is 1:30 [p.m.] here, and the next is 9:00 [p.m.] there and 3:00 p.m. here. If you get the phone call 7, 8 o'clock in the morning up at Davenport Street, where I live, "We want a piece from you today. We want you to film and cut a piece today." The day is very short. You can't start to get people before 9:00, offices open at 9:00. You're at scratch and you need to find the people to talk to, you need to go out and do it, you need to take some pictures, you usually do some vox-pops in the street with people. You probably need to do a stand-up yourself and to think out what to say and you need to get back here to edit the piece and to send it over on the satellite in time for the [7:30 p.m. show, which is] perhaps 1:30 p.m. here.

To give an example. They called me Tuesday morning wanting to have a follow-up story on Padilla [Jose Padilla, an American citizen with ties to Islamic fundamentalist organizations who was accused of involvement in a plot to construct a "dirty bomb"]. I was lucky to have a guy at George Washington University that I had used for a piece like a half-year ago, a law professor who's really good. He was there and he understood my lack of time, so I got to interview him early. And went out and talked to people in the street. And that was for the 9:00 [p.m.] news in Sweden, so we had the feed then at 2:15. It's a lot of work that has to be carried out in two to four hours from scratch to a cut piece. And it has to be good. You have to be accurate. You have to know what you're saying and make no mistakes. It's kind of a very demanding job.

Q: *Usually just with breaking news stories or does this happen more often than that?*

A: Usually with big news stories. But also it can sometimes be stories that are not so big here but would fit into a package over there that they are coming up with. . . . So what I would do would go together with another piece or two other pieces or a guy in the studio in Stockholm and they want to have the American aspect of something. It does not always have to be a breaking tremendous news story here in order to make me very busy, if you see my point. This happens often.

Patrick Smyth, *Irish Times* (July 22, 2002)

Smyth: I get up at half past 6:00, and I spend two hours reading the papers and surfing the net for stories. I read the *Post*, the *Times*, the *Washington Times*, and *USA Today*; all arrive by post. I subscribe to *Wall Street Journal Online*. Then I have to read the *Irish Times*. Magazines— the *Nation, New Republic, Time, Newsweek, New Yorker, Harper's, U.S. News*, and *Foreign Affairs*. That's a lot of reading. By half-past 8:00 I would be on [the phone with] my desk [in Dublin] to tell them what I want to write before they've got too many ideas themselves about what they want me to write. If I don't read the papers before I speak to them I'm at a distinct disadvantage. Then from 8:30 [a.m.] through to 1:00 p.m. I'm working on stories, on the phone or on the Internet, watching briefings on CNN, or coming in for an issue briefing. I have to file most inside page stories by about 2:00 p.m. After that a short break, then I will be working on longer-term projects or doing business, like arranging travel. Apart from covering the daily news, which can be two or sometimes three news stories a day, I would try and work on one more substantial feature.

Q: *Do you do a lot of analysis?*

A: I write a column once a week, which is a sort of "Letter from America," which can be analysis or sort of just about an issue. It's about 1,000 words, so it's quite substantial. The last was about how the business crisis is playing into politics, particularly looking at shareholders, pensioners, and how they were affected by the fall of the market. The last feature [was] on a book about new environmental economics based on the ideas of externalizing internalities, the idea of using market forces as a tool in environmentalism. And I went up to the Catskills to look at a major experiment where the water supply of a town is being provided by paying farmers to manage the water running through their land.

Q: *Do you ever do feature pieces on nonpolitical issues?*

A: Oh, yeah. Endlessly. Grisly murders and offbeat stories. It's the big sexy stories. Chandra Levy, which we followed at some length, unfortunately. The poor woman who killed her children in the bath, Andrea Yates. I find there is quite an appetite for death penalty stories, so I follow the death penalty quite closely.

Takeshi Yamashita, NHK-TV, Japan (August 2, 2002)

Yamashita: Yesterday was not usual. We had a live show. I got here at 9:30 [p.m.] and [the] live show [started] at 10:00. I didn't do the show, the bureau chief did. [But the show] featured my report recorded [beforehand]. I was covering the Senate hearing on Iraq. Then I wrote an article about the hearing. And then I had this party for some colleagues [from] Japan. If the editor wants to contact [us] or if we want to call [someone] in Japan, we have to call [around] midnight [here]. And yesterday I was at the party, and I [arrived] at the party at 10:00 p.m., then a little later I get a call [from my editor]. There is an FBI report . . . [*he pauses to think how to explain*].

Q: *The story that was in this morning's* Post *about the FBI and the WorldCom arrests?*

A: Yes. So they asked me to write an article. So I [did not finish] until 2:00 this morning.

Q: *Do you live nearby? You must have gotten home even later.*

A: I live in Bethesda, Maryland. And then they called me again at 3:00 [a.m.] because . . . in Japan, news has a . . . A few years ago, there was a case with [a group] who used sarin attacks. Do you know sarin?

Q: *You mean the Aum Shimrikyo attacks in the subways?*

A: Yes. Before the Aum Shimrikyo subway attacks, they [had committed] another crime. A man next to the crime site was suspected, and the media published his name. So did NHK. But [it turned out that] he was not related to the crime at all. So it was kind [of] a [media] human rights problem. So we are very prudent about reporting the person who is suspected. So in [the first draft of my article] I didn't write the names or the company, but Tokyo is more cautious, so they wanted me to [change some things in my story]. So they called me, and so I [finally got] to sleep at 4:00 a.m.

Chang Choi, MBC-TV, Korea (August 14, 2002)

Choi: We usually work in this bureau in accordance with Korea standard time. A lot of journalists here work in accordance with their own country's time. In the mornings we are free. We sometimes stop by some seminar, or we get a little bit of rest. Only after 2:00 p.m. [we begin working on] the news story, which [will be broadcast] in our morning news. Our morning news begins at 6:00 a.m. [in Korea], which is 5:00 p.m. in the afternoon here. So from 3:00 p.m. we prepare and see which story is better for the morning news story. So from 2:00 'til 4:00 and 4:30 we collect material, make a stand-up, and we write the story, do voiceovers recorded on the story. And we make a package with our stand-up, and we send it though this [*he gestures to machine*]. It is activated by the digital system. It sends almost instantly. So yesterday our main topic [was] the U.S. economy and how the U.S. economy influences the Asian market, Korea's money market.

From 4:50 [p.m.] through 6:30 I arrange the remaining jobs [that are not] news stories. In the news bureau there is a lot of extra work, management work. Then from 6:30 [p.m.] I monitor the evening news. CBS starts at 6:30. I monitor the news programs simultaneously, ABC and CBS. I turn up the CBS [sound] and turn on the captions on ABC.

Then I watch NBC news with Tom Brokaw [at 7:00 p.m.]. At 7:30 I round up the news of the day—what news can be worth broadcasting in the evening news time slot? So after 7:30 or 8:00 in the evening I call my editor in chief in my home country, and we discuss which story is best. I think three or four, average three, stories are picked as our nightly news items. So from that time, 8:00 [p.m.] to 1 a.m., I am working on the evening story. So I usually come into this office very late [in the morning] 11:00, 12:00. I am off Saturday. But Sunday afternoon, as you can guess, is Monday morning in Korea. So I can usually rest from Friday afternoon and Saturday.

Nobu Sakajiri, *Asahi Shimbun*, Japan (July 11, 2002)

Sakajiri: I don't have time to sleep. The daytime, for example, usually I wake up [at] 7:00, get down to [the] office, let's say 8:00 or 9:00 or 10:00 [a.m.] sometimes. I go to the seminar or briefing or symposium or something, I do an interview or read the newspaper. And around 5:00 or 6:00 [p.m.] we start writing the story: what happened today in Washington, D.C.

We have an international [section]; about from 10 to 30 percent is American news. Because even if [the story is about] the Middle East or Asian countries, [the editors] ask me to cover a story about the U.S. reaction. We recognize that the U.S. is the only superpower, so in every event we need what the U.S. government thinks about this. So the response from Washington is very important. Additionally, we cover incidents in the United States. So you can find many stories about the U.S. every day in the international pages.

We have two deadlines: 12:30 night and noon. At evening we file the story for [the deadline] at 12:30. After deadline, we very often start writing the story for the morning edition. And because 12:30 here, midnight, is lunchtime [in] Japan, they never hesitate to call us. [It is] very often 2:00, 3:00, or 4:00 o'clock until we have to stay here and file [the] story [before we can] go back [home]. I sleep maybe two or three hours every day.

Contact

Whereby the home office gains on correspondents

Contact between foreign correspondents and their home offices has expanded at a dizzying pace. "The CNN effect" was followed by something that could be called "the Google effect." Besides the quick and cheaper technology that has made interaction between distant reporters and editors possible and affordable, there is now so much more information, instantly available, that has to be weighed for its news value.

Quite suddenly the world of Korean television correspondent Chang Choi and his colleagues in Washington looked less comfortable. According to what Choi told us in 2002,

> The previous correspondents, before CNN was dominant
> in the world, they could sometimes lie to the editors. [They
> might tell their editors], "We can't do that. There's no
> material on that." But now with the Internet and CNN and
> all the information fed directly to our headquarters, with
> our foreign news department watching the video clips or
> all the information on the Internet . . . or they type in the
> keyword "Korea" on *New York Times* and all these stories
> come up on the screen. We correspondents are very
> concerned about that situation.[1]

More than one in four of the full-time correspondents said that their most recent story had been requested by the home office. Two in three had discussed the story with the home office before writing it, and nearly half had discussed the story with the home office after writing it. (Seventy-seven percent said that that was typical.) They also sent an average of eighteen work-related e-mails outside the United States every week, and some sent as many as eighty. The 20 percent of our survey respondents who were part-time correspondents had less continuing contact with the home office, although they reported that about the same percentage of their stories was suggested by editors.

Correspondents from virtually every country said that the leash between home and field was getting shorter. The rate of shortening was not equal, however. Europeans were held on the shortest leash, and the most tightly held were the French. Reporters for U.K. organizations told us that 22 percent of their story ideas came from London. The figure for German stories was one in three (33 percent). But nearly half (47 percent) of the French stories were requested by the home office. Complaints from the French correspondents were common. A magazine writer said that her editors' stereotypes "affect the choice of stories they would like me to write." A wire service reporter said that her "home office often wants stories confirming stereotypes about the U.S." A TV reporter said that his editors call for stories that "are more stereotypical" than he wants to write. A newspaper correspondent said that her editors "tend to like stories that show the extremes of American society—violence, political correctness, antiabortion movement, etc."

The CNN effect, as applied to foreign correspondence, is shorthand for the impact of global media outlets on editors in the home office, who dictate what their correspondents should be covering by what they themselves see and hear.[2] Only a few of the correspondents that we interviewed said that they were beyond its pull, usually for special reasons of experience or tradition. Concluded John Parker, Washington bureau chief of the *Economist:*

> In talking to my colleagues, I think I'm a real outlier. I have a totally different experience from them. . . . We are completely trusted. . . . We phone up every week and say, "This is what we're going to do," and they print it. They're not copy editors as it were—just making sure the commas are in the right place—but when it comes to the analysis of the U.S. from us, they leave us alone. . . . They almost never—in fact, I can't remember the last time they asked us to write a story which we hadn't suggested anyway, let alone asked us to write a story we thought actually completely stupid. My impression

from talking to my colleagues is that every day they're asked to write stories they might not otherwise have done.[3]

Henry Champ, a veteran Canadian Broadcasting Corporation correspondent, claimed that his long-standing relationship with his editors was symbiotic: "I'll be headed to the White House. I'll phone, as I did yesterday, and say, 'Listen, I just heard this report's coming out on the friendly fire incident.' They say, 'Yes, we saw that. We figured you'd be calling.' " The proximity of a common border greatly contributed to the arrangement, he noted:

> We have an editorship that's a little more knowledgeable about the United States than some other countries. [They're a] little more news nuanced. . . . Almost all of my editors know Washington fairly well. They've been back and forth. They've been to Disney World. They know . . . what the deal is. That makes it easier.[4]

In other cases news operations were simply too small to try to mirror CNN's coverage. Olga Bakova spoke of her editors in Bratislava, "They are not able [to keep up]. We have almost ten correspondents in the world at Slovak radio. If they followed everything, CNN or Russian TV, that's impossible."[5]

But most of the press corps claimed to have been on the short end of the CNN effect at some time. "It used to be, [when] I got here [in the early 1990s], they didn't have CNN yet all over," recalled Tom Buhrow, Washington bureau chief of Germany's ARD-TV:

> It was starting [to spread] after the Gulf War. It got really big. It used to be they basically couldn't control you as much. You had your raw material—you could get your wire sources, your pictures, your info, et cetera—and then they couldn't check it and compare it with their own viewing experience. Now, with CNN they got it running all the time. And you have to react to that, so that the pressure is bigger to [keep up with CNN].[6]

The television journalists, being in the same medium, felt the most pressure. Said Takeshi Yamashita of Japan's NHK-TV, "Always they are watching, and they get [ideas] from CNN and they call us. This is kind of embarrassing."[7]

On one level the complaint was that CNN and its cable rivals were distorting a country's selection of news. "Whatever happens, you get footage," said Swedish Television's Lars Moberg, "which makes the coverage of events in [America] overrepresented in our news."[8] Jorge Banales, of the Spanish news agency EFE, remarked:

> Today they [CNN] had another police [car] chasing a truck on a highway, I don't know where, and then the guy drove off the highway and crashed against a bridge, and that was all around the world. And then you will have an editor calling you to say, "Well, this story is on CNN," and I say, "Who cares?" So CNN is a curse for all of us.[9]

But most correspondents reacted primarily to the effect of the CNN effect on their own lives. Chang Choi, MBC-TV, Korea, commented:

> Our editors have no sense of distance and time. Even in the late night and early morning, like in the dawn time, they call me and say, "Check. Call the State Department now for confirmation." There is really no sense of time. And sometimes accidents happen in Ohio and broadcast on CNN. They see that in the daytime and pick up the phone and call me, "Go to Ohio." It's a very difficult situation.[10]

The difficulties that the CNN effect created for journalists deepened in the late 1990s with an explosion of news-related websites. "The CNN effect is not as important as the Slate effect," said Julian Borger of Britain's *Guardian,* referring to Slate.com:

> They send out an e-mail digest of the [American] morning press to a subscription [list]. So all of our editors have read the digest. They know what's the most important story in the *Philadelphia Inquirer.* They know what's in the *Boston Globe.* And when you wake up, and you talk to them at 7:00 in the morning, they've had a panorama of what's in the American press that day, so you are always behind them. You can't really pull any surprises on them.[11]

The correspondents' subliminal message, of course, was a standard complaint, a new wrinkle on an old theme—that editors were simply too oblivious to appreciate the subtleties of the correspondents' post or to comprehend the obstacles in their path. "My stories are based on insight my home office does not have," said Danish correspondent Lotte Lund Eriksen.[12] Yet there was no doubt that the playing field was tilting toward the home office. "They can read the *New York Times* from the Internet, you know," said Karin Henriksson of Sweden's *Svenska Dagbladet*, commenting on the morning exchanges with her editors on what she should be covering in Washington.[13] "The Internet is more dangerous [than CNN] because they can read the *Times* while I'm asleep," said Mike Hayashi, of *Yomiuri Shimbun*.[14]

Such remarks had to resonate in the foreign press corps when various previous surveys had shown that the *New York Times* was the reporters' number-one source of information. Charles Groenhuijsen, of NOS, Dutch radio and TV, noted:

We have a few guys back home who are very much interested in the U.S. And just like I do in the morning, they read the *New York Times, Washington Post, USA Today,* the CNN website, which is great. They have so much more access compared to twenty-five years ago. . . . The amount of information you have early in the morning when you come [to the office] in Holland—which is 3:00 a.m. here, and me waking up at 6:00 a.m.—is so much more [than before].[15]

Information is the editors' as well as the correspondents' stock in trade. Correspondents may be irritated because they have lost their monopoly on it and especially because their editors can soak up information while they are sleeping. But worldwide, around-the-clock, instantaneous television and Internet coverage enriches the amount of information available for their mutual purposes. By 1999 a full-time correspondent in the United States was spending nearly three hours a day on the Internet. And among sources for research—such as books, wire services, or the telephone—the Internet was rated most useful.

But how can one judge a source's reliability, and who is to be the judge? Yasemin Congar, Washington bureau chief of the Turkish newspaper *Milliyet*, commented:

They would call up at, say, 6:00 [a.m.] and say, "Have you read this?" and, of course, I haven't yet. They know more about what they're talking about now. And on the other hand, there are all these weird websites now. They would read something on the Drudge Report, and they would just think it [was a real story], sometimes really stories that are so absurd. Just because it's on the news they think there's some truth to it. They would make you work on it. [I try to tell them that] this is something, something-dot-com. This is not something you want to quote from, this is not credible . . . basically, you're wasting my time. If [they] really love the story, [I say that they should] use it, just say it [comes from] blah-blah-dot-com. Just don't make me [write about] it.[16]

Such problems, of course, are not unique to foreign correspondents. Albert L. May, in a comprehensive 2002 survey of the effect of the Internet on American political reporters, found that "to some degree" his respondents felt that "the Internet has inflated the number of rumors and bits of false information that make their way into the news." The trade-off was "a strong sense that the Internet has expanded the scope of journalists' sources, in both diversity and number."[17]

"Just do a search on the Internet," said Yasemin Congar. "You get so many different quotes that so-and-so told the *Los Angeles Times*. You don't even know that person, but the *Los Angeles Times* reported it on [its website] so it's [credible]. You don't necessarily use all that but you learn a lot." Yet because of the availability of the Internet and cable TV, she found that she was less likely to go to congressional hearings or Pentagon briefings: "CNN broadcasts Pentagon briefings. Why would you go to the Pentagon and sit there? . . . In a way it makes our lives easier, in a way less exciting and more boring. . . . Mostly what I don't like about my job is [that] it's more and more second-hand journalism." To Tim Lester of the Australian Broadcasting Corporation, "It's the media looking at the media looking at the media."[18]

British journalist Patrick Brogan, who covered the Senate Watergate hearings, concludes that the effects of CNN and Google—purely from the perspective of personal enjoyment—mean that "being a foreign correspondent here [in Washington] is less fun than it used to be."[19]

Access

Who sees whom, when, and why

Among our full-time correspondents, a substantial number—62 percent—complained that they had problems reaching sources because they represented non-U.S. news organizations. Many years ago, when Albert Hunt, then of the *Wall Street Journal,* was asked why Washington reporters always seemed to be complaining, he replied, "We complain because we are quasi-creative people."[1] But overall, the foreign correspondents that we interviewed were not notable complainers. Annette Moll probably reflected the feelings of the majority when she recalled being asked to cover Washington for German Public Radio:

> They offered me the contract and really it was, "Wow! [I can't believe that] they're offering me this." I think it's really the most prestigious job that can be offered as a media person. And yes, I gave up my apartment, I [sold] my car immediately [and said] "I'm going."[2]

"Of course, everyone wants to be a foreign correspondent in the U.S.," said Wei Tian, of China Radio International.[3] These were not unhappy people.

Yet this is a chapter about complaints. Our correspondents are complaining here partly because we asked them for their complaints, which generally related in one way or another to access. Still, some were quick to note that their access problem could be much worse, as did Rujun Wang, of China's *People's Daily:* "I think it's much easier than in other countries." He added, "I worked in India, I know everything about that. In India if you [want] to make an interview to some officer, that's unbelievable just because their [bureaucracy] is too slow. Here it is much better."[4]

Access, pointed out Yasemin Congar, "depends on the period, on who you are very much, on the issues, and on which agency you're dealing with."[5] It was access as affected by "the period" that Sabine Reifenberg, of German television network ARD, referred to in 1998 when she said that it had been easier for German journalists before the Berlin Wall came down and America's interests turned to other parts of the world.[6] "During the Clinton era, Russia was in fashion, so to speak," recalled Nickolay Zimin, of Moscow's *Itogi* magazine, in 2003. "It was much easier to gain access—if not to the secretary of state, then at least to Strobe Talbott. He was the deputy then and dealt with Russia, so you could also talk to other people through him."[7]

More dramatic still was the sudden access of Al Jazeera, the Arab satellite channel, after the terrorist attacks of 9/11. "In my personal experience," said Abderrahim Foukara in 2002, "if you're talking about people in the administration, most of the feedback I've gotten from my colleagues, who have been at Al Jazeera longer than I have, is that the administration is quite keen to talk to Al Jazeera and explain their point of view about whatever issue may be at stake."[8] However, with the founding of rival network Al Arabiya the next year, the Bush administration chose it as the more reasonable conduit to the Arab world, and the president granted Al Arabiya exclusive interviews in May 2004 (after the Abu Ghraib prison scandal) and in January 2005 (before the Iraq election).[9]

The list of those less fortunate would have to begin with correspondents from small countries that are not immediately important to U.S. strategic interests. "It's in our genes that we are from a small country," said Holland's Charles Groenhuijsen. "It's in our genes that nobody speaks Dutch. It's in our genes that nobody really cares." As for trying to interview members of Congress:

> We hardly try anymore. It's just hardly worth the time. I did an interview with [Senator] Joe Biden a couple of months ago because one of the spokespeople for Joe Biden is my neighbor across the street. I said, "C'mon, Norm, you owe me one." And eventually he arranged for it, and it worked out fine."[10]

Said Sweden's Karin Henriksson, "It's a rude awakening, I think, for many [foreign correspondents to realize that they are] less important than some local radio station, you know."[11]

The small-country problem was summed up by Olga Bakova, of Radio Slovensko:

> You have to be aware that you are from Slovakia and you cannot be the queen of the correspondents. . . . If Osama bin Laden was in Bratislava I'm sure I will have access to Colin Powell. I am not from those countries that are interesting right now. . . . Slovak Radio is one of the most trustful organizations in Slovakia, but I cannot explain this to somebody here.[12]

Indeed, correspondents' frustrations often were compounded when they thought of their employer as "the *New York Times* of my country," a perception mentioned to us by journalists from countries as different as Canada, Egypt, Singapore, Sweden, and Turkey.[13] "I don't want to judge," said Christina Maier of Germany's ARD-TV, "but the *New York Times* correspondent in Berlin would get much better access . . . and, in a way, for us being the biggest and most influential . . . I would expect a little bit more [access]."[14]

"Maybe if I worked for *Le Monde* or a paper like the *London Times*, but when you work for a little third world newspaper . . . ," said Betty Brannan Jaen of Panama, plaintively.[15] Oh, to have the access of the *Economist*—except if you happened to be Washington bureau chief of the *Economist*. Then the pecking order looked different. "The [domestic] TV networks, CNN, Fox, they're in first class," said John Parker, recounting press operations at the White House. "The main [U.S.] newspapers are in business class. And the foreign press is in steerage. And the *Economist* is sort of steerage plus."[16]

Occasionally a correspondent might get a little bump up when he or she was from a British newspaper with the right political slant. Julian Borger of the liberal *Guardian* noted that his competitor from the conservative *Telegraph* had been given an interview with President George W. Bush but that he himself had not. When pressed, he conceded that his paper had "had huge access to [President] Clinton."[17] Before President Bush left for London in November 2003, he granted an interview to the *Sun*. "Just to clarify," a British journalist asked White House press secretary Scott McClellan, "why has the president chosen to do an interview with the *Sun*? It's a newspaper which publishes daily pictures of topless women." "You should've seen the ones we declined," McClellan replied. But the correct answer, according to

Dana Milbank, was that "word on Fleet Street is it's an obvious payoff to the *Sun's* owner, Rupert Murdoch, the conservative publisher behind many Bush-friendly news outlets, such as Fox News." The headline over Milbank's story in the *Washington Post:* "Prez in Topless Tabloid; London Paper Nabs Rare Bush Exclusive."[18]

Some correspondents have niche access because they represent a country or a culture of special significance to the United States. Yolanda Sanchez of Mexico's Televisa cadged exclusive half-hour interviews with Ronald Reagan and Edward Kennedy when they were running for the presidential nomination in 1980. She told us that "a very large Hispanic audience" in the United States was the reason for her success.[19] Patrick Smyth of the *Irish Times* found that when "dealing with Congress there are different levels of interest in me. If there is an Irish story running, [legislators who are] friends of Ireland [will have their] press guys ring me back. I get hold of a congressman directly, they will speak to me, will want to speak with me. If I want to talk about anything else, it's a different bird altogether."[20] The experience of Carl Hanlon, of Canada's Global TV, was that members of Congress "who represent states which share a border with Canada are more willing to talk."[21] Rich Mikhondo, who reported for fourteen South African publications in 1997, remarked that members of the Congressional Black Caucus "are amazing for access. I can call Mel Watt (D-N.C.), and he answers the phone. I can just call Maxine Waters's (D-Calif.) office and speak to her."[22] "Working for the Vatican Radio helps, sometimes," said Paolo Mastrolilli.[23]

A remarkable instance of niche access was seen in 1987. While awaiting sentencing in federal prison, Jonathan Pollard, an American convicted of spying for Israel, refused all requests for interviews— except for one from Wolf Blitzer. Blitzer was the Washington correspondent for the *Jerusalem Post,* a small-circulation Israeli newspaper published in English. "He wanted me," said Blitzer, "because he knew my articles appear in Israel and they also appear in the United States."[24]

Reporters try to connect with the people in government who can explain the U.S. position on their countries. That is particularly important for journalists from small countries. "I focus really, really narrowly on anything that is happening in Washington that has a direct relevance to Panama," said Betty Brannan Jaen.[25] Asked if he knew the person who handled Greek affairs at the National Security Council, Dimitris Apokis, of *To Vima,* replied, "Yeah, he's a personal friend, very good friend. . . . We have common interests aside from the job, so we became friends and have a good relationship."[26] Said Pierre Steyn, of National Media of South Africa:

> I work mostly with the guys who work on Africa, so they have some idea of what's going on. If you go to the African sub-committee of the House, they know who Mugabe is, they know what the African Union is, that kind of thing. So I don't work with your run-of-the-mill congressman who probably couldn't find Malawi on a map of Africa.[27]

But the real complaints came when correspondents talked about their efforts to interview Mr. or Ms. Big. "If I got an interview with Condoleezza Rice, that would obviously be big," said Karin Henriksson. "But if I got an interview with her assistant, the deputy national security adviser, that wouldn't really play out as big, even though it's almost the same thing, because he's not well known outside Washington really."[28] This was a major problem for the Japanese. Said Nobu Sakajiri of *Asahi Shimbun*, pointing to a series of poster-size photographs in his Washington bureau:

> Look at this. This is the former president of my company [*with President Reagan*]. And that one is a former bureau chief [*with President Clinton*], and that is also [a] bureau chief [*with President George W. Bush*]. So this kind of opportunity is very prestigious for [our company] and for the journalists themselves. So, how do you say . . . for the bureau chief the only duty is to get the interview with the president. He can spend one year or two years here [working] to get the interview with [the] president. Once the other competitor got the opportunity, it will be seen as trouble for the bureau chief [because] this is why he's here. [The news business] is very competitive in Japan.[29]

An opportunity to interview the president usually came—if it came at all—in advance of a president's visit to the correspondent's country. And thus it happened for Lars Moberg of Swedish Television in 2001, along with Washington correspondents from Spain, Belgium, Poland, and Slovenia:

[State department officials] assembled us for a meeting ahead of the interviews to give us the format and to give the rules. . . . It was absurd in a way that you're getting a one-on-one, an exclusive interview with the president of the United States, and they tell you that it's going to be very brief, very short, three minutes. And we yell and we say, "Hey, but three minutes. You can't do an interview in three minutes. I mean, what's three minutes? Nothing." What if I put a question and he would just filibuster and give me a long dried-out answer that didn't really say anything and then, "Thank you. Next."? We tried to protest as loudly as possible but we couldn't change it. And, of course, everyone was still happy about the fact that you would interview [the president of the United States]. . . .

When you get there, in the White House, I couldn't bring the cameraman that I work with, the staff cameraman. The White House provided everything. They would give you make-up, but done by the White House. And they would line us up. You walk into the room—a room crowded with people—and there's Bush sitting in a chair. He didn't stand up and say hello. It was just, because of time, it would be too time-consuming that he would rise and talk to everybody like that. So he was sitting there, and you have three cameras— one camera on the president, one on me, and one double shot. So then you have all the technicians for the cameras and the lights. Then you have Ari Fleischer, you have Karen Hughes, and you have these people lined up. So it's a crowded room and there is the president waiting. And when you're going to start the interview, you say, "Hello, Mr. President, how are you doing?" Then a guy behind the camera over there says, "Swedish Television, all right, go, you have *two minutes.*" And they promised three minutes, and I couldn't start arguing at that point with Bush sitting there, but I managed to squeeze out three minutes anyway. I managed to put a very brief question when that guy was waving a stop sign. I went on, and as soon as Bush answered, they couldn't stop him [from answering my question], so I felt very good it was done.[30]

White House, Pentagon, and State Department briefings were the most persistent cause of correspondents' complaints. Tim Lester of Australian TV had this to say:

> I imagine the White House could very easily pull out a book and say, "Hey, White House correspondents come here daily. You guys don't. You're only occasional turn-ups." And that is an issue. There's a pecking order here in Washington that I haven't struck anywhere else in the world. If you're at the White House press briefings, then there are certain key U.S. media organizations that get their questions answered first, which makes it more difficult to get your questions answered, which is fair enough—I mean, the president needs to worry about the American people first and foremost. There's nothing wrong with that. I just want to get my question about [some] Australian thing in too. It's difficult to get questions in.[31]

Christina Maier of Germany's ARD-TV offered another illustration of the access problem:

> Let me tell you a little anecdote about the press conference with Mr. Rumsfeld at the Pentagon. We do have access to the press conference; unfortunately, we don't get a question because he always asks other people. One day I really wanted to get a question in. So I went there, which we don't even do anymore usually. And I [call out], "Mr. Rumsfeld." No, he didn't see me. And then [I call out again], "Mr. Rumsfeld." And I'm getting more and more [insistent] . . . "Mr. Rumsfeld, Mr. Rumsfeld. Hello!" It took ten times and only because I really shouted and I shouted louder than anyone else. He finally [called on me]. [He was] probably wondering, "Who is this [obnoxious] European lady?"[32]

Adnan Aljadi, of the small Kuwait News Agency, had a more benign view of life at the daily briefings:

> You go to briefings, and if you're not called on you keep going and listening. It's a good experience. . . . I don't think any really good journalist would say that attending briefings

is a waste of time. You just go there and see what happens. Something good might come out.[33]

But for a few, such as Christophe de Roquefeuil of Agence France-Presse, the French wire service, the job came with a reserved seat in the front row:

> My position is very specific. I am basically a State Department correspondent. I spend most of my time in the press room of the State Department. . . . The State Department makes a clear difference between the regular correspondents like me, who are everyday, every week, at the State Department [and those people who just drop in]. And the State Department and diplomats and press officers, they are very sensitive to that. If you are spending most of your time with them, among them, in any activity, big news, small news [they keep you in mind]. The State Department rewards people for being regular attendees.[34]

Yet were the regulars the equals of their domestic counterparts? Jim Anderson, who had been the State Department correspondent for an American wire service, United Press International (UPI), switched employers and went to work for Deutsche Presse-Agentur (DPA), the German wire service. After he retired, we asked him whether it made any difference. His reply:

> Not really. Partly because the State Department press corps is fairly small, and it doesn't make much difference whether I'm representing DPA or UPI. I know the same people, both in the corps and within the State Department, and they know me personally. The difference is that at UPI I used to get a lot of floated stories handed to me. You know, policy stories. It was common. If the State Department wanted something out it had to give it to UPI and the AP. So we often were just handed stuff before anybody else got it. That doesn't happen with DPA. DPA is not one of the kingpins, so you have to work a bit harder for it. Also, a lot of the stories that I chased [for DPA] were different than the ones that I chased for UPI. Obviously UPI was mainly interested in a domestic American audience. For DPA I had to think in terms of a worldwide

audience. Some of the stories that used to be very important—changes in personnel within the State Department—would simply not be useful for DPA. I probably had less success as a DPA reporter in getting telephone calls answered than I did for UPI. That's partially because with UPI they knew that whatever I put out would be coming across the State Department teletype within minutes. It would be seen in the operations center and would get on the secretary or the assistant secretary's desk within half an hour. They [the State Department] don't monitor DPA that closely. The monitoring is done only in Germany by the U.S. embassy, and so once in a while a story would get some attention, and once in a while I would get a leak, a guided story from the European bureau of the State Department, which wanted to bring a story or a policy to the attention of the German government.[35]

In the highly stratified White House press corps, a small group of reporters, some of whom represented foreign media, were both regulars and outsiders. They showed up each day at the press secretary's briefing, and their presence caused controversy. Reporters from the major U.S. outlets called them "the foils." According to Dana Milbank, "The use of foils, a technique popularized by Clinton press secretaries Mike McCurry and Joe Lockhart, involves the careful selection of questioners from among the many raised hands to steer the briefing in a direction the press secretary desires."

In the *Washington Post*, Milbank described a session in January 2002 when the reporters wanted to talk about the Enron scandal and Bush press secretary Ari Fleischer did not. The "foil" was Raghubir Goyal of the *India Globe*, who usually asked about "the perfidies of Pakistan":

> [P]eppered with questions about Enron . . . , Fleischer turned to the Goyal foil. "Goyal," Fleischer said, as others shouted to get his attention. Fleischer said to the others: "We'll come back. We'll come—we'll—"
>
> The press corps resisted. "Ari?" one called out. "Let me follow that, Ari—"
>
> "Hold on," the press secretary commanded. "Goyal, go ahead."

Goyal did his usual. "If I may go back to India and
Pakistan . . . ," he began.[36]

In 1978 Carl Leubsdorf of the *Baltimore Sun* had written a similarly
disparaging article about a group of reporters whose questions at
White House briefings also were at cross-purposes with the primary
needs of the mainstream press. One of the offending journalists, John
Szostak, who wrote for Polish newspapers, sued Leubsdorf for libel in
the District of Columbia small claims court. (Szostak lost.)[37]

While those are extreme examples of relations between the foreign
and domestic press corps in Washington, they do suggest tensions at
some levels. Comparing life as a foreign correspondent in France with
her experience in Washington, where she worked for *Arab News* of
Saudi Arabia, Barbara Ferguson said, "The other thing in Europe that
was really good fun is that we would share information. If somebody
missed a briefing, not a problem, they'd fax the notes to you. We'd sit
down after a briefing and talk over what we'd thought about it. Here I
find that American journalists keep everything very close to their
chests."[38] "This is very stereotype and generalization, and I know this
is not fair," said Jorge Banales, a Uruguayan who works for EFE, the
Spanish news agency. "So when you are in a group and you go to cover
State Department, any briefing, first of all you have to deal with your
own [press] colleagues who are American and they don't think that
you [as a foreigner] are a journalist."[39] Such comments, even if they
were rare, described those beats where reporters were forced to spend
the most time together and hence became the most clannish.

For those for whom access was most difficult, there was always the
government's Foreign Press Centers. Patrick Sabatier of *Liberation*,
France's largest newspaper, viewed the centers as an "American propaganda machine."[40] But they were deeply appreciated by those of less-
elevated station, such as Envera Selimovic, a Bosnian journalist, who
was lent a television camera when she was in need.[41] Or Olga Bakova
of Radio Slovensko:

It's really [the] best institution to have, 'cause they will help
you, tell you where to go, what to do. Mrs. Liza Davis, she is
really great. Even if I call her or try to e-mail her [to get help
to understand U.S. political institutions] she has immediate
answers. Which is really great, 'cause these kinds of political
institutions are different from Europe.[42]

There was also access to interviewees-for-hire, experts in politics and public policy who were paid small sums—usually in the $100 to $500 range—for their TV and radio comments. Yuko Fuse, a Washington reporter with Nippon Television Network (NTV), said, "We don't like to pay fees for news, [but] sometimes [it] could happen. There's a long tradition of gift-giving in Japan. Fees are considered part of that."[43]

And ultimately, there was access to the American people, who, unlike their government, got high marks. "People in general speak more openly in the United States than in other countries," said Eugen Freund of ORF, Austrian Radio and Television.[44] "Sometimes Americans are almost more willing to discuss a delicate or personal issue with a foreign journalist," thought Chilean freelancer Lydia Bendersky, "because they know that no one in the United States will see the story."[45] Concluded German radio broadcaster Annette Moll:

I have to say that more often than not the people here are better than the ones I would get in Germany because grammatically German is a more complicated [language]. It's much longer, and [in America] people have a way of expressing themselves that's much less stilted, not convoluted or technical. . . often very good for sound bites. They really know the art of . . . to make short sentences with a funny note, a sort of ear-catcher.[46]

Help

Foreign correspondents as clients of the U.S. government

"The most valuable help I got from them was probably
when they put me in contact with prison staff who
could arrange interviews with convicted murderers for a series on
violent crime, something that would have been virtually impossible
on my own as a foreign journalist," recalled Gunilla Faringer, a
reporter for Swedish newspapers in New York.[1]

The "they" that she remembered were the men and women who
work for the Foreign Press Center, a tiny unit of the U.S. State
Department with offices located in Washington, New York, and Los
Angeles. Seven people work in the New York office on East 52nd
Street, two in Los Angeles, and thirty at the National Press Club
building in Washington, eight of whom are program officers
responsible for a particular portfolio of countries. "The mission" of
the centers, according to a State Department brochure, "is to support U.S. policies and priorities by helping resident and visiting
foreign media cover the U.S."

Official government support for foreign journalists began in
New York in 1946 when hundreds of journalists arrived to report
on the newly founded United Nations. A second center was opened
in Washington in 1968, and a third in Los Angeles in 1982, when
Californian Ronald Reagan was president. Peter Kovach, who
directed the centers in 2002, explained their roles:

> Washington is the hub of government news; New York
> tends to generate stories focused on economic issues, cul-
> tural issues, and UN politics; while the L.A. center focuses
> more on Pacific-rim politics, Silicon Valley news, Holly-

wood entertainment reporting, economics, and even a large contingent of Japanese baseball writers shuttling back and forth from Seattle to cover the exploits of Ichiro Suzuki.[2]

In 1999, 79 percent of the 219 Washington respondents to our question on use of the Foreign Press Centers (FPC) said that they had used the center in Washington; 59 percent of the 167 New York respondents had used the New York center; and 28 percent of the forty-three California respondents had used the Los Angeles center. That the centers were outposts of the U.S. government did not appear to bother the correspondents. "There is no doubt in my mind that the FPC promotes, or at least guards, the American government's line," Dutch journalist Tim Overdiek told us. "It would be very naïve to think otherwise. But that's okay. As journalists, we are smart enough to see through all this and make our own analysis in regard to information we receive."[3] Or, in the words of Nadia Tsao, a Taiwanese reporter, "We are sophisticated enough to tell information from propaganda."[4]

Advances in technology had altered the character of the FPC by the time of our study. Gone was the coziness described in a 1986 *Washington Post* story: "part workroom and part social club . . . a mother lode of information not to be mined elsewhere."[5] Only a few correspondents—like Greek freelancer Dina Pinos in New York—still dropped by to "use the phones, the library, the magazine information, watch the news, get the papers."[6] Most relied on their own computers. "The thing is that the Internet has taken over so much information that you do not need to use the center that much," remarked Norwegian reporter Finne Thurmann-Nielsen.[7] Ian Brodie of the *London Times* recalled that he used to visit the Washington center "sometimes every day during [a] crisis when Marlin Fitzwater's White House briefings [during the Reagan and George H. W. Bush presidencies] were piped in. That changed when [President Clinton's press secretary] Mike McCurry allowed cameras at his briefings and they were picked up live by CNN and C-SPAN."[8]

My research assistant, Daniel Reilly, spent Friday, February 15, 2002, at the Washington center clocking its use by visitors: at 10:34 a.m. three correspondents were there; at 10:39 one more arrived; and at 10:40 one left. By 10:51 one correspondent remained. According to Reilly's log,

His name is Stefano Marchi and he works for *Il Tempo,* an Italian daily. He is the quintessential FPC user, as he is a contributing writer for the paper but does not have an office. He claims, "I couldn't survive without the FPC." He uses the FPC support materials for "every" story he writes.

At 12:35 p.m. Reilly struck up a conversation with Nickolay Zimin, correspondent for *Itogi*, a Russian weekly magazine:

> He describes in detail how the FPC was much more crowded back in 1992 when he arrived in America, how before the Internet the FPC was much more of a gathering place for foreign media. He tells me he has a computer at his home; he usually only comes to the FPC on Fridays to read newspapers and occasionally meet with the FPC staff.

The general consensus, as stated by French correspondent Jerome Godefroy in New York, was that "the FPCs are very useful to foreign correspondents with small resources or for those who just arrived in their U.S. assignment."[9] Those distinctions were apparent in interviews with the Washington center program officers. George Newman spoke of helping newly arrived African journalists face a myriad of challenges, while Katherine Turpin spoke of the limited needs of the "low maintenance" veteran Western European correspondents that she served.[10]

Beyond one-on-one assistance, often related to problems with visas or press credentials, the centers are responsible for on-the-record briefings, mostly with high-ranking officials. There were eighty-six briefings in 2001, thirty-nine of them by the State Department. The following were some of the speakers and topics for the month of January:

—Ed Gillespie, "Presidential Inaugural: Themes and Events"
—Norman Ornstein, "The New Administration and the New Congress"
—Richard Holbrooke, "Tenure as U.S. Ambassador to the United Nations"
—John Zogby, "A Pollster's View of Election 2000"

Other topics addressed during the year were more specialized: Bosnia-Herzegovina (May 15); the humanitarian situation in Sudan (July 12); HIV/AIDS trends in Asia and the Pacific (October 26); and tracking the financial assets of terrorists (December 4).

Attendance ranged from ten to fifteen for what Peter Kovach called "boutique briefings," such as those on the environmental implications of the drug war in Colombia, to 130 for the best-attended briefing, a session with President Bush's chief economist. The sign-in sheet for a March 12, 2002, briefing by Alan Larson, under secretary of state for economic, business, and agriculture affairs, speaking on "The Monterrey Conference on Financing for Development," showed forty-eight correspondents from the media of twenty-one countries, including ITAR-TASS (Russia), Agence France-Presse, Al Jazeera, and NHK (Japan).

When we polled the correspondents on the usefulness of the briefings—with 5 being *most useful* and 1 being *least useful*—the average ranking was 3.09. Correspondents' explanations of their rankings varied:

—"I'm not interested in the briefings or events which have no direct relation to the Indonesian issues."[11]

—"They are more print press–oriented. We are trying to cut back on 'talking heads'."[12]

—"The problem is that when you work on a daily deadline, sometimes you don't have time for a briefing, unless the subject is exactly the hard news of the day you are covering."[13]

—"The Foreign Press Center has a habit of arranging briefings at mid-morning, which is mid-afternoon in London, and the point at which my deadline is approaching. Invariably I am unable to break away."[14]

Foreign press briefings appeared to be given higher priority as Iraq and terrorism became the government's dominant concerns. Among those who made the trip to the Washington and New York centers in 2004 were Secretary of State Colin Powell; General Richard Myers, chairman of the Joint Chiefs of Staff; and FBI director Robert Mueller.

In addition to briefings, there were press trips. These included a visit to upstate New York to see an "entertainment complex" owned and operated by the Oneida Indian Nation; a trip the Humana Festival of New American Plays in Louisville, Kentucky; a visit to witness the "behind-the-scenes workings of a congressional office" with Dennis Kucinich (D-Ohio); a preview of the Olympic Games in Salt Lake City; a tour of the Pentagon during reconstruction after the September 11 attack; and a trip to the North Slope oil fields in Alaska. Our respondents gave the trips an average ranking of 2.73 on the 1–5 scale. As one respondent wondered: "Why don't they ever plan trips to earthquake areas, tornado areas, hurricane areas? Why not a trip to the new gated communities that are popping up all over America? How about a trip to Wyoming after the Laramie gay murder?"[15]

The FPC also organized "thematic tours," which Jefferson Brown, the Washington center's director in 2002, called its "growth industry." This program brings journalists to the United States for short periods; candidates are proposed by U.S. embassies around the world and subsidized by the government. Reilly reported to me,

> Brown sees these tours as invaluable, as the special behind-the-scenes itineraries designed specifically for foreign journalists help "capture the nuances behind our policy much better." He cites the overwhelming success of a recent tour highlighting the Muslim experience in America, taken by Indonesian journalists. By taking these journalists from Washington to Dearborn, Michigan, by introducing them to average American Muslims, top officials at the White House, and top-level Muslim clerics, Brown felt that the tour helped "to show [the journalists] a reality that probably doesn't match the preconceptions that an average Indonesian would have about American society."[16]

The embassy in Jakarta agreed. A long internal cable dated February 2, 2002, advised the secretary of state:

> SUMMARY: TWELVE INDONESIAN JOURNALISTS FROM MAJOR NEWSPA-
> PERS AND MAGAZINES TOURED WASHINGTON, D.C., DETROIT AND
> DEARBORN, MICHIGAN, AND NEW YORK CITY FOR TWO WEEKS ON A
> FOREIGN PRESS CENTER PROGRAM TO LEARN HOW THE SEPTEMBER 11
> ATTACKS AFFECTED THE U.S. AND TO OBSERVE ISLAM IN AMERICA. . . .
> ALMOST 30 ARTICLES HAVE BEEN PUBLISHED TO DATE AND THESE
> ARTICLES HAVE BEEN BALANCED AND OVERWHELMINGLY POSITIVE. IN
> FACT, THESE ARTICLES HAVE BEEN THE BEST SERIES OF ARTICLES ABOUT
> THE U.S. IN MEMORY. . . .

The translated articles that we were shown supported the embassy's assessment. In *Sabili,* which the FPC described as a "radical Islamic" magazine, there was a low-key report on March 21, 2002, in which the writer told of a conversation that he had with two Muslim West Point cadets:

One of them said that terrorists had misinterpreted the meaning of jihad. . . . "In fact, the Prophet said that we are returning from a small war [jihad] to a bigger war [jihad], that is the jihad against lust," he said. In other words, jihad, according to this American Muslim cadet, is a war against lust. I said this hadith is very popular in Indonesia. . . . The expression that "jihad is a war against lust" is a good one.

After the 9/11 attacks, "public diplomacy"—efforts to influence public opinion in other countries—was tapped for a more prominent role by the Bush administration. The experiences were rocky at both the State and the Defense Department. Charlotte Beers, a well-known advertising executive, was named under secretary of state for public diplomacy and public affairs, but her slickly produced media campaign aimed at Muslim countries—called Shared Values—was considered a disaster by Arab experts, and she quietly resigned in early 2003. She was replaced by Margaret Tutwiler, a former ambassador to Morocco, who, in turn, was replaced in early 2005 by Karen Hughes, the president's close adviser. At the Pentagon a newly created unit, the Office of Strategic Influence, was accused of planning to place "disinformation" in the international media, and it closed after a few months. The Foreign Press Centers continued their low-key efforts to help journalists.[17]

Modest efforts were made to help foreign journalists by groups outside the federal government. So-called "international press centers" (IPCs) were established in Chicago, Cleveland, Houston, and Seattle. (An IPC was said to be in Atlanta, but we could not find anyone at home after repeated tries.) Three of the groups were run through Chamber of Commerce–type organizations, while the Chicago operation was a desk in the city's tourism office. The people in charge at each IPC told us in 2002 that their work with foreign correspondents took between 5 and 10 percent of their time and that they helped between thirty and fifty visiting journalists in a year. The Seattle IPC was the exception: it averaged between sixty and one hundred journalists. The extra interest in Seattle was created by the presence of Microsoft, Boeing, and baseball's Ichiro Suzuki. Interest in Houston related to the energy industry. Cleveland's story was urban renewal: "Imagine politicians of diverse ideologies who trash one another every day joining hands with top entrepreneurs of their region to make their city a better place to live in," began an account in the *Times of India*.[18]

The IPCs in Chicago had little to offer resident correspondents, explained Gerardo Cardenas, of Notimex, the Mexican wire service:

> Since there are very few foreign journalists based in
> Chicago—about ten, including myself—there's little Pat
> [the IPC director] can do for us, other than an occasional
> phone chat or helping us locate an elusive source. Chicago is
> quite easy in terms of accreditations. Other than the police
> and the mayor's office, and you don't really need those if
> you're not local, no other public institution issues press cre-
> dentials. And the ones issued by private concerns (sporting
> teams and the sort) are easy to get. So that's another area in
> which the international press center can't really help you.
> Since Pat does not have enough budget, she can't organize
> press briefings. And if she did, who would brief and who
> would come?[19]

Finally, there was help for foreign journalists on various websites, such as the International Journalists' Network (IJNet), designed to point the way to grants and programs that offer study or training in the United States.[20]

Borrowed News and the Internet

Where correspondents turn for information

The connection between reporters and their home offices was not the only aspect of foreign correspondence that was being profoundly changed by the Internet. "Online [access to information] has revolutionized the speed and breadth of research," noted the BBC's Philippa Thomas.[1]

Journalists are great consumers of journalism, hence the term "borrowed news." Most of the Washington reporters we surveyed in the late 1970s read four newspapers a day, and our foreign correspondents in the late 1990s averaged the same number. But newspaper consumption for foreign correspondents is much more important, especially if they do not speak the language well or have not been in the country very long. Indeed, some foreign correspondents say—not entirely in jest—that they are only as good as the local press.

By 1999 the Internet had pulled slightly ahead of newspapers in foreign correspondents' rankings of their most useful resources.[2] That did not imply that correspondents had stopped reading newspapers, only that they often read them online. Ninety-one percent of full-time correspondents reported that they used the Internet to do research, 81 percent to check headlines, 80 percent to read foreign media, and 71 percent to read U.S. papers.

Full-time correspondents spent nearly three hours a day on the Internet. Less than 5 percent of irregular correspondents were nonusers, ranging in age from 73 to 93, plus a younger writer who covered opera for a Hungarian publication and a Senegalese specialist on immigration. (See figure 1, page 102, for number

FIGURE 1. Number of Newspapers Read and Hours Spent on the Internet Daily by Foreign Correspondents, 1999[a]

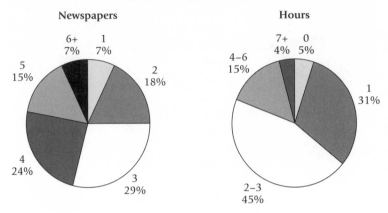

Newspapers   Hours

a. Number of respondents: newspapers = 415; hours = 425.

of newspapers read and hours spent on the Internet daily by correspondents.)

The *New York Times* and the *Washington Post*, which are published in the cities where most of the correspondents lived, had the greatest readership, 89 percent and 70 percent respectively, followed by the *Wall Street Journal* (54 percent), *USA Today* (31 percent), the *Los Angeles Times* (17 percent), the *Washington Times* (16.5 percent), the *New York Post* (10.5 percent), the *Financial Times* (10 percent), the *New York Daily News* (8 percent), and the *Christian Science Monitor* (7 percent). The correspondents were attentive magazine readers: *Time* (64 percent), *Newsweek* (63 percent), the *Economist* (24 percent), *U.S. News & World Report* (24 percent), the *New Yorker* (24 percent), and *Business Week* (16 percent). Fifty-two percent listened to National Public Radio. Very few correspondents indicated that they watched the TV Sunday interview programs.

An assumed consequence of the journalists' reading habits troubled Ambrose Evans-Prichard, a conservative correspondent for the *Spectator* of London, who wrote in 1988, "This kind of derivative journalism, of which I am just as guilty as anyone else, involves repackaging stories from the two great liberal papers: the *New York Times* and the *Washington Post*. The effect is insidious. . . . By relying on the *Post* and the *Times* (as well as TV network news, which strikes me as an electronic cousin) for most of their information and insights, foreign correspondents are essentially picking up a Democratic point of view."[3]

Evans-Prichard's contention was not tested by our survey (if it could have been tested), but when we asked correspondents where the idea for their most recent story came from, eleven of 415 respondents said the *New York Times*. Those stories tended to be "soft stuff" or features, on topics such as "young people who quit their stressful jobs and work for less money" (for a Spanish newspaper), "new video game aimed at Christian market" (U.K. newspaper), "music over the Internet" (French wire), and "Robert De Niro's plan to build a movie studio in Brooklyn" (Argentine magazine). Three correspondents borrowed one story idea each from the *Wall Street Journal, Los Angeles Times,* and *Washington Post*. The *Post's* contribution to foreign correspondence was a tale about the pandas at the National Zoo (Japanese TV). The primary sources for the government variety of breaking news were "the wires," AP and Reuters.

It was not the ideological slant of the mainstream media that was important to foreign correspondents—President Clinton would hardly have agreed that the press was his political ally—but rather that the press had become increasingly oppositional to the sitting president, particularly in matters of foreign policy—and that provided foreign correspondents with abundant dissenting material.[4]

The Internet gave correspondents wider, faster, and cheaper access to the nation's newspapers than they had when we first looked at their reading habits in 1979. Did this make them less dependent on the "insidious" influence of liberalism that worried Evans-Prichard? The 1999 evidence was that most news—borrowed or not borrowed—overwhelmingly came from New York and Washington papers (including the conservative *Washington Times*). Those who said that they read the *Boston Globe, Chicago Tribune, Newark Star Ledger,* or *Miami Herald* could be counted on the fingers of one hand. Papers from nineteen other cities—including Anchorage, Salt Lake City, and Minneapolis—had a reader or two.

Yet it was as a research tool, not a tool for serendipitous sampling, that the Internet added value. Christopher Reed in California went to the websites of "all the main metro papers west of the Rockies," which was the area he covered for British and Australian publications.[5] Martin Kettle, reporting for the *Guardian* (United Kingdom) in Washington, sought local papers when national news happened in their area, citing "*Denver Post* [regarding] Littleton shootings."[6]

There was some interest in magazines of opinion: thirty-one respondents read *Foreign Affairs* or *Foreign Policy*; twenty-eight, the *New Republic;* and twenty-five, the *Nation.* Ten read at least one of the conservative magazines (*Weekly Standard, National Review, American Spectator,* and *Insight*). A correspondent for a Lebanese paper said that the idea for his story "U.S.-NATO Separation: Ground War or Path to Peace?" came from the *Nation.* More typical of the magazine-inspired stories were ones about model Lauren Bush, the future president's niece (for a French magazine) and "gender-specific brain differences" (for German TV). The correspondents' tastes were broad but not deep, favoring the sort of magazines found in a supermarket rather than a college bookstore.

Despite the influence of the CNN effect in directing coverage to events such as plane crashes and killer tornadoes, only one correspondent, writing a business story for a Swedish paper, claimed that the idea came directly from television. However, another story idea was a multimedia creation: the reporter saw a TV account of a magazine article—"Hillary Clinton's Remarks about Her Husband"—and wrote it up for a Brazilian newspaper.

How the Internet altered the way that correspondents conducted their research depended on their needs, computer skill, and sophistication. Juurd Eijsvoogel, a reporter for *NRC Handelsblad* (Netherlands), explained that his first online stop was the *International Herald Tribune* because it appeared "earlier on the net than the *New York Times* and *Washington Post,*" the paper's co-owners in 1999, and he then used the *Washington Times* for the "daybook," its excellent listing of events in the capital.[7] Luis Costa Ribas, a reporter for S.I.C. Television (Portugal), explained: "Instead of calling a source looking for information, I first search the Web, read what's available, and then start calling people up for interviews and the like."[8] Some looked for what one correspondent called "great links." Herman Y. C. Pan, of Taiwan's Central News Agency, used the Drudge Report website for "AP, UPI, Reuters, AFP altogether."[9] Freke Vuijst, a Dutch TV journalist, used the website of the *American Journalism Review* for its links to "regional newspapers."[10] The websites that Gerardo Cardenas, a reporter for Notimex (Mexico), used most frequently were those for Newswise, Eureka, the *New York Times,* Yahoo, HotBot, Electric Library, Bloomberg, and the Library of Congress, as well as Internet publications *Slate* and *Salon.*[11]

Correspondents' specialization affected where they went for information. Correspondents in New York covering Wall Street chose websites such as EDGAR (U.S. Securities and Exchange Commission), First Call (company earnings reports), Forrester (technology research), and NAPS (business press releases). Washington correspondents were more likely to mention PollingReport.com and PoliticalJunkie.com or DiploNet and embassy.org. A Hollywood reporter said, "I'm in the habit of hovering above chat rooms devoted to a certain theme whenever I have to write something specific that needs a bit of street flair."[12] But most simply listed the big portals, like Yahoo and Google.

The correspondents' experiences in surfing the Web, both in terms of time spent and expansion of the diversity and number of sources, resembled the online experiences of the American political reporters that Albert May interviewed in 2002.[13] The Internet had the same advantages and disadvantages for all journalists, foreign and domestic. But for foreign correspondents it was also their means of keeping on top of developments in their own countries. Correspondents read their own newspapers every day; many also read the opposition. The correspondent from Mauritius read the three papers from her country.[14] Arab journalists read Israeli papers. Taiwanese journalists read Chinese papers. The Washington correspondent for Brazil's *O Globo* read his paper, two other Brazilian papers, Mexico's *Reforma*, Colombia's *El Tiempo*, and Argentina's *Clarin*.[15] Others got a broad sweep of news from their country or region, with at least one correspondent citing such websites as allAfrica.com, CANOE (Canadian Online Explorer), Edicom.ch (French-speaking Switzerland), GlasNet (former Soviet Union), LANIC (Latin American Network Information Center), Nifty Serve (Japan), Paperball (Germany), Sahafa (Middle East), SINA (China), and Sunet (Sweden).

When we began this study, these connections were not available to correspondents, who sometimes lamented being out of touch with their audience—or, in other cases, did not seem to notice. Those who wanted to keep in touch had to rely on regular mail delivery and occasional trips home. While, as previously noted, correspondents now lamented the degree to which the Internet allowed the home office to look over their shoulders, it was equally true that the Internet operates in both directions. The correspondents' access to their own publications was more than a comforting connection for those who might yearn for the latest cricket scores. It was also a constant reminder of subtle changes in their company's product that could affect their work and position.

The Internet deposited incredible amounts of information on correspondents' desks, C-SPAN presented the U.S. Congress in session, and other cable channels offered White House and State Department briefings. The American media were rich in insights and opinions that were there to be borrowed. The government tried to be helpful, up to a point. Those were no small blessings. It was increasingly possible for foreign journalists—whose access may be limited, whose budget may be modest, and who may be working against the clock—to cover their beat without leaving the office, especially in Washington. But as with all new technology, there is always the flip side. For those who contend that what distinguishes journalism from other forms of information gathering is "shoe leather," the loss of first-hand experience and personal observation is not inconsequential.

What
They Report

"The release of the three American soldiers will at best lead to the release of the two Yugoslav soldiers held by NATO but will not end the bombings. On the other hand, Clinton pronounced for the first time the word 'cease-fire,' not so much to test diplomatic waters but more so because he was asked in a very direct manner in the presence of the Japanese prime minister."

—Klaus Jurgen Haller, West German Broadcasting,
May 4, 1999

"Milosevic agreed to free the U.S. infantrymen after an emotional meeting with a group of religious leaders headed by American civil rights leader Jesse Jackson. Dr. Nazir Khaja, the president of the American Muslim Council in Washington, accompanied Jackson. . . . 'I must say that it is a moment of great pride and pleasure to be part of this team effort,' Khaja said."

—James Flanigan, Kuwait News Agency,
May 9, 1999

"Everything hangs on one word, the word 'pause.' This is the first time that Bill Clinton has evoked such a suspension of bombings. The chief of the White House accompanies this word with numerous conditions. It would be necessary that the Serbs effect a start to withdrawing their forces from Kosovo. But the word has entered the American vocabulary. Jesse Jackson, returning from Belgrade, came to plead before his friend Clinton the opening of dialogue."

—Jerome Godefroy, RTL French Radio,
May 3, 1999

"Serbia and Kosovo can end up being an infernal trap for NATO countries. This is because if bombs and missiles will not succeed in stopping Belgrade's dictator, what will be the next political-military option? . . . Joseph Nye, professor at the Kennedy School of Government, Harvard University, usually conservative in his forecasts, depicts the scenario as follows: 'Americans look at the horrible things that happen around the world and say, "Something needs to be done," but we're not sure about the price that we want to pay. Thus they don't pay attention to the fact that some of these problems can be solved only on the ground and not by air.' This means that soldiers and tanks need to be sent to face a war that could otherwise end up being a disaster. For both Milosevic and for NATO."
—Antonio Carlucci, *L'Espresso* (Italy),
April 8, 1999

"So the bombing campaign continues in what could be a long war of attrition:
"Major General William Nash (retired), former U.S. commander [in] Bosnia: 'By choosing this route we have forfeited the opportunity for a decisive victory and we have, in fact, accepted the fact that we will negotiate a settlement.'
"Anthony Cordesman, military expert: 'Does this mean NATO inevitably wins? No, it doesn't. Does it mean Serbia can simply hide? No, it can't. And this problem of how to predict the outcome of the air war remains just as uncertain.'
"[Correspondent]: But most military analysts here are making one prediction with a great deal of certainty. They say that any final settlement of the Kosovo war will be a compromise—one in which Milosevic may have to make the biggest concessions, but NATO too will have to dilute its war aims."
—David Halton, Canadian Broadcasting Company,
May 19, 1999

One Day

The stories and the categories that they fit in

We sought answers to the questions of who foreign correspondents are and how they report from the United States, but another question remained: what do they report? Each day produces hundreds of thousands of words in scores of languages. Gathering and translating them would be no small task.

Some U.S. government agencies—the CIA, the State Department—create daily transcripts of reports in the world media, but those transcripts are too selective to answer our question. Do Washington embassies retain and translate their country's newspapers and magazines? No such luck. Much of the world's media have websites, but they are too idiosyncratic for comparative analysis. Commercial translating was too expensive for our budget.

The best solution that we could come up with was simply to ask the correspondents to tell us about their most recent story. What was the subject? How long was it, in words or seconds? Where did the idea come from? What events were attended, interviews conducted, or documents or other sources used in order to write it? Was the home office involved? Was the story typical of the correspondent's work? We also asked for a copy or tape of the story. (An SOS then went out to our colleagues at Brookings for help with translating.)

We received 415 usable responses from journalists representing sixty-one countries.[1] All the responses were not returned on the same day, unfortunately. Still, we choose to think of them collectively as "One Day: Foreign Correspondents' Reports from the United States."

There always will be "breaking news," stories that must be reported. At the time of our 1999 survey two events dominated the news, skewing coverage in their direction: the air war in Kosovo, especially civilian casualties and the bombing of the Chinese embassy in Belgrade by a U.S. plane on May 7, including a quick trip to Europe by President Clinton, and the aftermath of the fatal shooting of twelve students and one teacher by two fellow students at Columbine High School in Littleton, Colorado, on April 20, with renewed debate in Congress over gun control legislation and a quick trip to Littleton by President Clinton.

Stories were assigned to one or more of five categories: Culture (including movies, museums, media, sports, travel, art, theater, books); Government: Domestic (relating to actions on the federal, state, and local levels by executive, legislative, and judicial entities); Dangers (guns, drugs, crime, accidents); Private Sector (business and the economy, science and technology); and Government: International (foreign policy, diplomacy, military). The "home angle" was noted in all categories. (See figure 1, page 111, for percent of stories in each category.)

Nearly a quarter of all stories (23 percent) were related to culture, a quarter of the culture stories were directly related to the movie industry, and a quarter of the movie industry stories were about *Star Wars.* "Panned by Critics, Assailed by Fans, the Film Arrives in a Hysterical America," read the May 19 headline of France's largest-circulation newspaper, *Liberation.*[2] Its Washington correspondent, Patrick Sabatier, began the story, "*La Guerre des étoiles . . .* , George Lucas's intergalactic saga, is for certain the most-awaited film in the history of cinema, indeed an event 'equal in importance to the new millennium,' as it has been proclaimed in the media." Toru Takanarita, also from Washington, wrote in *Asahi Shimbun,* "The Star Wars story speaks to the times as hundreds stand in line for weeks for an opening-night ticket."[3] Another quarter of the movie stories were celebrity interviews, with, for example, Calista Flockhart (Australia), Sandra Bullock (Finland), Charlize Theron (Denmark), Anthony Hopkins (Thailand), Will Smith (United Kingdom), Natalie Portman (Switzerland), Kevin Kline (Italy), and Rod Steiger (Serbia). No country seemed immune to the tales of an actor with a film to flack. Even when the locale wasn't Hollywood, correspondents were drawn to the movies: there was a report for an Indian magazine on a children's film festival at the Asia Society in New York; a Colombian paper's account of the Human Rights Watch

FIGURE 1. Subject of Foreign Correspondents' Most Recent Story[a]

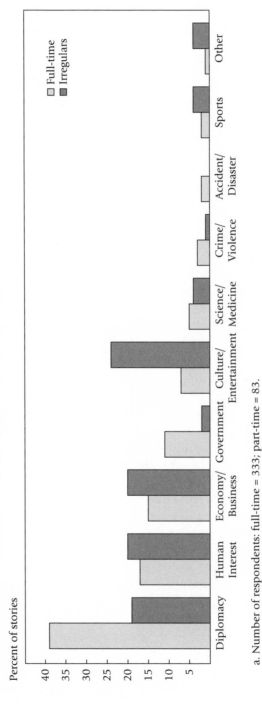

a. Number of respondents: full-time = 333; part-time = 83.

Film Festival, featuring a Colombian movie; and an article on another New York film festival, this one about films from Portuguese-speaking Africa.

If movies were not the subject, then television—or, more broadly, the media—was. A Swiss newspaper wrote of "the power of television images" in the reporting on Kosovo.[4] French television focused on "the responsibility of the media in covering the Clinton sex scandal."[5] A Japanese wire service wrote about efforts to regulate "violence in the media." ("I've always been interested in the media," explained the Japanese correspondent.[6])

The home angle in this category included a segment for German TV on German actors working in Los Angeles and an interview of a Greek director in New York for a Greek newspaper. The graduation of a Taiwanese girl from the Virginia Military Institute was a big TV and print story in Taiwan. There were also success-in-America stories that were sent back to Finland, Hungary, and Sweden. A nanny who won $197 million in the lottery in Boston earned an eight-page cover piece in a Chilean magazine. A four-minute segment on *Vremya*, ORT/Russian Public Television, was the ultimate home angle story:

> **Correspondent Vladimir Sukhoi:** In this house, standing on the corner of Hope Street in Providence, is the Thomas Watson Academic Institute of International Research. The institute is a part of Brown University, the pride of the smallest American state, Rhode Island. But Sergei Krushchev is the pride of the institute and of the university because he is the son of the former First Secretary of the Central Committee of the Communist Party. Nikita Krushchev once promised to bury America. Sergei Krushchev lives in this America, and now he has filed a request [for] American citizenship.
>
> **Sergei Krushchev:** It seems to me that the cold war has ended. I live here. And the difference between Russia and America is simple. As Famusov said, 'My house is open to the invited and to the uninvited, and especially to foreigners.' In Russia it is good to be a foreigner. But in America, the American citizen stands in the first place.[7]

There were travel pieces about Florida's Key West and Manhattan's East Village; baseball stories for Japan (pitcher Hideo Nomo's comeback) and basketball stories for Lithuania, whose correspondent said "basketball is the second religion in Lithuania,"[8] and an article on the "rising popularity of women's soccer in the United States" for Nigeria.[9] Coverage in the culture category was generally upbeat. Canada's CBC did a radio story in French on the falling pregnancy rate among American teenagers. The single exception was a Portuguese TV segment about "abandoned children in New York."[10]

What distinguished the culture category from the others was that a third of the output was written by irregulars and another third by full-time freelancers, which suggested that such stories were less likely to appear in the major mainstream outlets that have their own correspondents in the United States.

Domestic government accounted for 11 percent of the stories. When sorted by level of government (federal, state, local) and by type (executive, legislative, judiciary), almost all of them were about the national government and almost half of those were about the presidency—or, more precisely, about running for president, even though the next presidential election was a year and a half in the future. "Rivals Struggle to Halt Bush Juggernaut" was an eight-column headline in the *Sunday Telegraph* (United Kingdom), June 13, 1999. In the *Edmonton Sun* (Canada), June 20, Patrick Harden wrote from Washington that Al Gore, "being an unapologetic supporter of Clinton throughout the interminable embarrassment of the Jones-Lewinsky scandals," has "baggage he'll have to unload in the next few months, and it won't go easily." Other presidential contest stories appeared in newspapers from Argentina, Denmark, Italy, Mexico, Norway, Poland, Spain, and Sweden; on French and Swiss radio; on Egyptian and Korean television; and on Mexican and Spanish wire services. There was one story about Elizabeth Dole's campaign, by Kathleen Kenna of the *Toronto Star*.

Congress was the subject one-quarter of the time. Most of the stories were about gun control legislation and Senate rejection of the Comprehensive Test Ban Treaty. There also was a report on Chinese nuclear espionage by Helge Ogrim, Norwegian News Agency, on May 26, entitled "Hunt for the Guilty after Spying Allegations." It begins: "Republican politicians demand Democratic blood after the report by Congress on the theft of U.S. nuclear secrets by the Chinese. Some are demanding that Attorney General Janet Reno step down. . . ."

The judiciary figured in only three stories. Because "Brazil is reforming its judiciary system," *TV Cultura* asked its New York–based crew for a five-minute segment on "the American judiciary system."[11]

A Finnish reporter described his story as "Death Penalty in Illinois, Innocent People Released from Death Row."[12] And the Chicago-based correspondent for the *Economist* did a piece on a Michigan trial in which the jury ordered Warner Brothers, owner of the *Jenny Jones Show*, to pay $25 million to the family of a gay man, a guest on the show, who was later killed by another male guest after revealing on the air that he was sexually attracted to him. The conclusion: "It would be ironic if a tawdry show like *Jenny Jones* has a lasting impact on American law." The story was suggested by the home office.[13]

The states were almost invisible in the reporting—there was a 2,500-word article about Minnesota Governor Jesse Ventura that focused on his drug policy, for a Dutch newspaper. However, there was no shortage of speculation on whether Hillary Clinton was going to run for the U.S. Senate from New York, a topic that generated stories in Russian, Portuguese, and Brazilian newspapers, in a German magazine, and on an Egyptian wire service.

Government at the local level was also nearly invisible: there was one article on public schools in a French magazine for the intelligentsia and another on a "controversial antigang ordinance in Cicero, Illinois" by the Chicago correspondent of a Mexican wire service.

There were two home angle stories. Reporting for the *Philippine Daily Inquirer* on July 19, Jennie L. Ilustra traced a delegation that had come to Washington to lobby members of Congress for pension benefits for "some 60,000 surviving Filipino World War II veterans with nonservice-connected disability." The other was "Congress Denying Money to Families of Calalese Victims," about restitution for those killed when a U.S. military plane flew into an Italian ski lift. It was "the leading story of the day," said Andrew Visconti of L'Espresso Publishing Group—"one of the best assignments of my career."[14]

As if to help explain why 11 percent of the stories fell into the dangers category, on May 16, Martin Kettle told his *Guardian* (United Kingdom) readers: "Seven more people were reported dead last week in the worst heat wave in years. . . . In some areas water is running short. . . . But all this is happening in India, so you don't really want to know." Kettle offered a number of reasons why a similar disaster would be news if it happened in the United States: "The U.S. media [would] set up the live coverage and [do] the interview. The rest of us [would] regurgitat[e] it." His major conclusion: "Perhaps the truth is that the British secretly enjoy transatlantic misfortune too much. Perhaps, in an era of U.S. global hegemony, they secretly need to be reassured that

their masters are gun-obsessed crazies or that their lovingly con-
structed Oklahoma suburban homes can be smashed to smithereens
within seconds by some arbitrary force of nature. Serves them right for
being top nation."

On May 4, the Australian Associated Press carried this, combining
the topic of danger with a home angle:

> A storm cellar and a bathtub sheltered two Australian women
> for several terrifying hours when powerful tornadoes touched
> down near Oklahoma City yesterday. Pamela Singleton of
> Sydney took shelter with her family and neighbors in an
> underground storm cellar located in the back yard of her
> home. In the relative safety of the cement room she watched
> the tornado live on television as it headed for her house.

And on May 21, the Turkish Anatolia News Agency, ran the
following:

> Coming to Littleton from Turkey together with his family a
> year and a half earlier, Semih Altnay explained, "Two students
> with weapons started chasing as many as 100 students out-
> side." He recalled, "I saved myself by escaping and hiding
> under a desk in a classroom . . . from there I heard gunfire
> and at least one hand grenade explode. . . . You never would
> have expected this kind of incident in a school like this.
> Columbine is a very good school. There weren't even fights
> here."

(Other Columbine stories were produced for television in Austria,
Canada, Germany, Japan, Portugal, and Sweden.)

Two other stories combined the topic of danger with the home
angle: a Mexico newspaper account of Mexican drug cartel operations
in the United States and a Spanish wire service "interview [on] death
[row] of a Spaniard sentenced to the electric chair" (with photos).[15]

Twenty percent of the stories concerned the private sector, a category that was divided between science and technology stories (20 percent) and business and economy stories (80 percent). The
science/technology stories were one of a kind, some significant, some
frivolous, without a discernable pattern: climate change (Venezuela),
dinosaurs (Argentina), tobacco additives (Norway), pandas (Japan),

leprosy (Germany), medicinal mushrooms (United Kingdom), genetically modified materials (Netherlands), experimental space shuttle (France), power outages (Canada), and breast implants (Finland).

Twenty-six countries produced business/economy stories, but nearly one in five was written for Japan; no other country was a close second. Few of the Japanese stories had a home angle. Their focus was on aspects of the economy rather than on business deals: the "U.S. economy's strength, related to GDP"; "bankruptcy," concerning the progress of congressional legislation; the "U.S. retail industry"; "day traders"; and "online trading." The correspondents reported that they had done multiple interviews, attended a number of events, and used many documents in writing their stories.

Most other stories were comparable to what is found on the business pages of an American paper: AT&T's layoff of workers; Korean companies on the New York Stock Exchange; the Florida real estate market in an area favored by Finns; Goldman Sachs's initial public offering; the Microsoft trial; recession in Hollywood; the Alitalia-Northwest merger; the euro-dollar exchange rate. Home angles included the sale of two French champagne makers to a private Dallas investment company (*Les Echos,* May 4) and a report on wine conventions in New York (Agence de Presse, May 24): "Alice Loubaton, senior product director of food and wines from France . . . noted that 'there is no other major trade exhibition like this in New York. We felt the need.' Looking at the thousands of people on the floor smiling, sipping, and spitting, she said, 'This puts a face to products and makes it easier to sell.' " Correspondents also chronicled a feast of conferences on U.S. companies investing in Africa, India, Romania, and Russia.

The most stories, 35 percent, concerned international government (foreign policy, diplomacy, and military affairs), reflecting the shift of correspondents from New York to Washington, although the UN was a bigger player than usual during this period. Many of the accounts could also be labeled "relations," as in U.S.-China relations, U.S.-India relations, U.S.-Japan relations, U.S.-Korea relations, U.S.-Taiwan relations.

May 1999 offered the foreign press corps a bonanza of stories in Washington and New York. NATO was holding a fiftieth anniversary celebration in Washington. As a result, Macedonian TV would interview the president of Macedonia, and Finnish TV would interview the president of Finland, and the Bulgarian correspondent would go to dinners and press conferences and meetings with the Bulgarian dele-

gation. In New York, there was the signing of the East Timor Autonomy Plan, a story of immense importance to Indonesian and Portuguese journalists. At the White House, President Clinton met with
Prime Minister Keizo Obuchi of Japan, the biggest story of the year for
the large Japanese contingent but also major news for China and Taiwan. Home angles included visits from the British secretary of state for
Northern Ireland, the Canadian foreign affairs minister, and the prime
ministers of Norway and Taiwan.

On Kosovo, the big breaking news story, there was little evidence
that the correspondents' digging went much deeper than borrowed
news. Of fifty-five reports, only ten included enough independent
material, such as interviews or documents, to suggest that the correspondents were doing more than relaying information from wire
services or major U.S. outlets. There were exceptions. Philip Klint of
Eco News (Mexican TV) reported on "the faces of some of the Kosovar
refugees who in the last forty-eight hours have been welcomed by U.S.
officials at Fort Dix military base in New Jersey," and on May 10, 1999,
Ian Brodie had a front-page story in the *London Times,* reporting from
Whiteman Air Force Base:

> Americans have never fought a war this way before. B2 pilots
> take off after dawn from the Missouri plains to bomb
> Yugoslavia. They are home the following afternoon, after
> 30 hours of non-stop flying, in time to see their children play
> soccer and have dinner with their families.[16]

Not all countries were equally interested in having their correspondents produce home angle stories. Major Western European
media appeared least likely to consider this type of news a significant
part of their responsibility. That may reflect what Michael Rice has
called the "cosmopolitan ideal" of "a great newspaper," citing the
Frankfurter Allegemeine Zeitung, the *New York Times,* the *London Times,*
and *Le Monde* as rising above "a narrow nationalism."[17]

Of 157 stories in the French press, just four were home angles:
three were about the U.S.-French disagreement over the Yugoslavia
embargo, and the fourth was an interview with American writer Stanley Karnow about his book *Paris in the Fifties.* Seven of twenty-seven
German correspondents wrote home angle stories. A German radio
reporter described his story: "U.S. Congress discusses gun laws, [I]
compare the measures with the much stricter gun laws in Germany."

The seven Spanish correspondents filed two home angle stories among them, one about the Broadway musical "Rent," which was about to open in Barcelona, the other about a Picasso exhibition in New York. Only the British media continued their "special relationship" with the United States, with ten of twenty-one correspondents writing at least one home angle story. The *Telegraph* ran three about a British nanny on trial in San Diego in the death of a baby.

It was almost a rule of the road that the smaller the country, the more engaged its correspondents were in finding the home angle. A Finnish correspondent filed a story about a reunion of Thomas Jefferson's descendants, some of whom had Finnish blood. According to a survey respondent, "Normally, one of four stories has a Norwegian reference."[18] "You always try to find an angle that can make Swedish readers feel involved."[19] Other countries also fit in this category, for example, Guatemala, Nigeria, Portugal, South Africa, and Turkey, although the relatively few stories could have reflected the predilections of particular correspondents.

Still, for another set of countries—not defined by size—exploring their country's relations and connections with the United States ranked as their media's most important business. On that list were Mexico, Canada, Taiwan, South Korea, and Israel and the surrounding Arab countries. These nations' interest in American government policy was not casual. Canada and Mexico are U.S. neighbors. "Our major objective here is covering Mexican issues in the USA," said a newspaper correspondent.[20] Such issues were largely political events in Washington and New York, cities with relatively small Mexican communities; as noted during a 2003 journalists' symposium in Tijuana, there was little coverage of the 9 million Mexicans in the United States or the 23 million Americans of Mexican descent.[21] Fifty-nine percent of Canadian correspondents' stories were of the home angle variety, covering everything from bankruptcy filings by Canadian companies in the United States (*Toronto Globe and Mail*) to results of a survey on how Americans feel about Canada (*Toronto Star*) or simply putting a Canadian spin on a U.S. event, as in the *National Post:* "Pat Buchanan—the Republican firebrand who denounces free trade, supports smokestack industries, and is suspicious of Canada's liberal image—announced his intentions to run for the Republican presidential nomination yesterday."[22]

Eighty-three percent of stories for Taiwan focused on the home angle, 80 percent for Israel, 73 percent for Kuwait (50 percent for the whole Middle East), and 57 percent for South Korea. Happenings in America were so finely sifted by the media of the Middle East that a story in *Arab News*, Saudi Arabia, reported that former Israeli prime minister Binyamin Netanyahu was having a "tough time getting pricey speaking engagements in the U.S." (The correspondent listed the story as coming from "word of mouth.")[23]

Ultimately, then, "One Day: Foreign Correspondents' Reports from the United States" produced stories on this mix of topics: international government (35 percent), culture (23 percent), the private sector (20 percent), domestic government (11 percent), and dangers (11 percent), with the prominence of culture stories, as noted, probably overrepresented in our sample. The frequency of home angle stories varied from country to country; they were least visible in western Europe. What deserved more attention—or less? The main reason that other countries' media invested scarce resources in reportage about the United States was not that the United States was amusing or strange or colorful. It was that the United States—ally or enemy, buyer or seller, benefactor, polluter, or merely sideline spectator—was important to them.

Now

What we know about foreign correspondents in America, the present

When our story began in 1955, foreign correspondence often appeared to be defined by an elegant web of special relationships between America's economic and governmental elites in New York and Washington and a coterie of well-bred Western European journalists: Marino de Medici, whose ancestors had their portraits done by Botticelli, from Rome's *Il Tempo*; Herbert von Borch, of Munich's *Suddeutsche Zeitung*; Werner Imhoof, the intellectuals' favorite, from *Neue Zurcher Zeitung*; Adalbert de Segonzac, Ziggy to his friends, reporting for *France Soir*; the urbane Alistair Cooke, explaining the meaning of "TV dinner" to his BBC listeners; and Henry Brandon, of the *London Sunday Times*, who missed his regular Sunday tennis game when his partner, the U.S. national security adviser, had to attend to the Cuban missile crisis.

A generation later, membership in the club of foreign correspondents no longer seems quite so exclusive. Why? What happened?

—*The numbers.* In 1955, when Donald Lambert did the first scholarly study of foreign correspondents in the United States, he located 250 correspondents, "the total number in this country." By 1964 there were 616, and there were close to 2,000 by the end of the century. The foreign press corps has grown beyond coziness. But it isn't just the numbers. It's who they are, where they come from, and what they do.

—*Gender.* A 1970 survey by Chung Woo Suh reported that the foreign press was 95 percent male.[1] While women still remain a distinct minority of full-time correspondents in our survey—

only one in four—they make up half the population of part-time correspondents.

—*Location.* Western European correspondents continue to dominate, but not quite as much as they once did. In the course of a generation—1964 to 2000—they increased threefold, but during the same period, Asian correspondents increased fivefold. Western Europe's share declined from 54 to 47 percent of all foreign correspondents; Asia's share rose from 17 to 27 percent. The great rush came from Japan.

—*Television.* Much of the increase in the foreign press corps comes from television. In 1961 only nineteen television and radio foreign correspondents were members of the Congressional Press Galleries; in 2002 there were 458. The presence of the camera affects both the style of the Washington scene and the content of the news as stories become even more events-dominated.

The direction of these changes—many more correspondents but a smaller percentage of print-oriented, white, male, European correspondents—contributes to producing a foreign press corps whose denizens are not as likely to be invited to supper in the family dining room at the White House. The decline of salon journalism—of the Walter Lippmanns and Joseph Alsops, of off-the-record chats with the secretary of state in Georgetown drawing rooms—is evident in the U.S. media as well. As government expands beyond the capacity of those "in the know" to adequately serve all information-seekers, many of the same complaints about access are heard from domestic reporters, whose numbers also have multiplied, with the result that the foreign correspondents simply take their place at the back of a longer line.

An irony, perhaps, is that the one group that can sometimes jump the queue is a rag-tag bunch of writers for the world's movie fan magazines—the Hollywood Foreign Press Association—who invented a marketing gimmick that the industry needs, the Golden Globes, and now get special sessions with celebrities. Presumably, too, when a greater share of box office revenues comes from overseas, the Hollywood foreign press will be loved even more.

For most foreign correspondents—those who are never invited to play tennis at the White House or to sup with movie stars anyway—how much has really changed over the years? Senators and ranking officials may snub some of the journalists who are big shots in their own country (or least work for their country's leading news organization), but there are plenty of folks in universities, think tanks, trade associations, and the Foreign Press Centers who are ready to help. And there is a lot of U.S. journalism that can be borrowed, even though borrowing becomes more dangerous when the home office has access to the same material on the Internet. Most correspondents are experienced professionals who know the limits of their own influence and only wish that their editors understood those limits better.

Yet this was not an unhappy press corps. Quite the contrary. Of the three cities where, for the most part, they congregate, Los Angeles is congenial and close to the beach, New York is cosmopolitan, and Washington produces a steady stream of events of international significance. Regardless of any disagreements they had with the U.S. government, they overwhelmingly found the United States a good place to live and raise a family.

There will always be correspondents of the traditional mode, who cover New York or Washington for three or four years before being reassigned to Moscow or London for a similar tour. By our calculations, only 16 percent of the press corps now fits in that category, suggesting that our early concern about the need to examine "rotation policies"—whether they are too long or too short—is less relevant now. In organizations where it still matters, the preference of those in our survey for a four-year assignment—the length of a presidential term—makes sense, at least for correspondents in Washington.

Clearly another personnel pattern is emerging. Mainstream operations are using a U.S. assignment—especially one in Washington, which has replaced New York in terms of importance in the news—as a one-time foreign posting. More than half of the press corps comes directly from the home office, although some have had other overseas experience. These journalists are punching a ticket on the way up in their organizations. They are on the fast track, and they will return to headquarters (probably permanently) to work as editors on the foreign desk or as executives, commentators, or TV anchors. (It is hard to believe that this practice is a phenomenon only in the United States. It must apply to postings in other capitals, since it would be odd to move correspondents around the world without including an American assignment in the mix.) The change may reflect the reality of personnel management in a world of working spouses. It may reflect one notion of how to distribute limited foreign assignments more equitably. It may reflect the relative value to an organization of foreign and domestic jobs. If it provides a glimpse of the future, it reflects a trade-off whose consequences are not yet clear. The downside is that journalism loses a breed of world-circling correspondents whose experiences add a richness and understanding to their reporting that cannot be replicated by brief overseas tours. The upside is that journalism gains home offices with more built-in knowledge and awareness of the rest of the world. The new pattern, however, does not reflect doing business on the cheap, because it is cheaper to move correspondents and their families as few times as possible.

Doing correspondence on the cheap requires hiring contract workers. Maintaining a foreign bureau is expensive. At commercial enterprises, how much money is spent on foreign correspondents depends on the balance sheet, while government-run or -financed news operations can be held hostage to the state of the national economy, political pressures, and competing demands for resources. In setting priorities, decisionmakers take into account consumers' interest—or lack of it—in far-off places. News organizations know that they can fall back on wire service stories that they receive through paid subscriptions. For companies under constant pressure to find ways to cut costs, another solution is to employ writers who already are in the United States and others who will work for piece rates.

Full-time "local hires" amount to 20 percent and full-time freelancers to 12 percent of the foreign press corps in the United States. Local hires are less likely to stumble over the peculiarities of the American political system, such as how to matriculate in the electoral college. But they also are less likely to weave their employer's country into their stories. Are there differences in attitudes and law on gay rights, abortion, and divorce, for instance? A challenge of reporting from another country, writes an Irish correspondent, is "to find resonances of home in the strangest places."[2]

Moreover, 20 percent of those that we surveyed were not full-time journalists; they were the irregulars, who sell occasional pieces to overseas outlets. The freelancers and irregulars, who often hold other jobs, may have a personal agenda, perhaps unknown to the editors buying their material. They also are less likely to share the stereotypes of the United States that may be fashionable in the home office. Their stories, often cultural in content, enrich and expand the usual menu that organizations get from their own correspondents, who tend to be tied down to breaking news and the top stories of the day.

All major changes in foreign reporting during this period were products or byproducts of changes in technology. From the correspondents' perspective, the changes contributed to their loss of control over information in their organizations. When our story began they had a near monopoly on reporting from the United States and many other locales and on its relative importance and interpretation, limited only by budget.

The foreign press, especially in New York, expanded greatly with the creation of the UN after World War II and the emergence of the United States as a cold war superpower. From the 1940s into the 1980s, correspondents were nearly independent operators. In the United States, they tended to be of long tenure, thus acquiring expertise and thereby a shield against second-guessing within their organizations. That was promoted by the type of journalism they practiced, analytical pieces that could survive slow delivery, usually by mail. The high cost of communicating with the home office, via cable or telephone, helped to minimize field-to-headquarters contact.

By the early 1990s, dramatic coverage of the Gulf War—generating what became known as the CNN effect, the ability of home office newsrooms to view events around the clock, often in real time—started to increase editors' interest in the United States, the scene of many of the stories, and to sharpen their views of what their reporters should be covering. At the same time, the Internet increased the ability of editors and producers to direct their overseas correspondents; depending on the time zone, some had access to the day's editions of newspapers such as the *New York Times* before their New York correspondents even woke up.

The increased quality and reduced cost of long distance telephone service, along with e-mail, vastly increased the interaction between headquarters and correspondents. That applies to all news staff, not just those overseas—to interactions between London and Manchester, Paris and Bordeaux, New York and Los Angeles. But if, as the Barber dictum states, "Happiness is in direct proportion to one's distance from the home office," that type of happiness is leaking out of foreign assignments—although some correspondents grudgingly admit to benefiting from supervision.

Different organizations react differently to the reduced proximity between headquarters and field. Some very small operations have too many pressing problems to try to micromanage faraway staff. In others, the prestigious job of U.S. correspondent is awarded to such esteemed staffers that they continue to retain considerable autonomy. Most autonomous is the esteemed staffer from a small country. In general, the more important (and larger) the news operation, the more intrusive the direction of its foreign bureaus.

The desire to direct foreign staff varies with the importance of the country to which they are assigned. Those reporting from small countries probably still experience benign neglect on the part of their editors; those in the United States are kept on the shortest leash. How short a leash has a lot to do with relations between the two countries: using correspondents to perform a bit of America bashing can be a great temptation. Initially this phenomenon was most apparent in our interviews with French correspondents; it turned global when Iraq became an issue. A report from the American Institute for Contemporary German Studies in August 2004 observed: "Some Washington-based reporters . . . found it very difficult to convince their editors to run stories that did not buttress the image of a unilateralist, united America bent on conducting a devastating war against the tenets of existing international law."[3]

As if having editors looking over their shoulders isn't bad enough, the new technologies allow—virtually require—correspondents to respond faster to events. Technology shrinks the time between happening and reporting. If the event is important enough, radio and television reporting has to be in real time.

The Internet makes reams of information—and misinformation—instantly available. It broadens the fact base of reportage. Suddenly there are wondrous new sources to be quoted—as well as banana peels on which to slip. It can also tether correspondents to their computers, limiting the time that they have to go out and fraternize with the natives. Journalists once stopped by the Foreign Press Centers to read newspapers and magazines or watch closed-circuit White House and State Department briefings, activities that they now do more efficiently alone at home or the office. So the centers are no longer a surrogate social club, a place to go for enlightened exchange and gossip.

Moreover, the Internet can actually reduce the correspondents' advantage on some types of news—stories about U.S. economic activity, for example. Given government and commercial databases, how much difference does it make whether the correspondent is in New York or in Frankfurt?[4] The clarity and relative affordability of worldwide telephone service also puts foreign correspondents in competition with home-based reporters. As any "source" in Washington knows, the next call could just as easily come from Buenos Aires or Moscow as from an office in the National Press Building.

Advances in air transportation—now fast, available, and affordable—are quantified in the greater number of cities visited by reporters. In a country the size of the United States, that translates into improved coverage, notably by television journalists, who now can travel more often with lighter, more compact equipment. The ease and speed of world travel also presents news organizations with an excuse for further cost-cutting, as seen in companies that replace permanent foreign bureaus with parachutists (less politely called "day trippers") to give a publication or program an international veneer without making a major investment. For really important events, headquarters can bypass resident staffers and dispatch its "Big Foot," even the TV anchor. Hundreds of journalists from around the world descended on California to watch Arnold Schwarzenegger become governor; Canada's *Globe and Mail* even sent a correspondent to describe the media descending on California.[5] A Sacramento paper interviewed a radio reporter from the candidate's hometown of Graz, Austria, who complained that Schwarzenegger's stump speech on "leadership" would translate as *fuhrerschaft,* an ominous word in German. "I'm just going to say he's calling for lower taxes," she said.[6] And what Japanese journalist would not want to be in the United States to see Ichiro Suzuki make baseball history by breaking the record for hits in a single season? The consequences of globalization can work in strange ways for foreign correspondents in America, especially when the dollar is a bargain.

After years spent observing them, we could not help being sympathetic to the men and women of the foreign press corps: they work long hours, often reporting to home offices in distant time zones; they struggle to overcome language or cultural differences that make understanding complex stories more difficult; they have limited access to big shots who don't think that they have anything to gain from talking to them; they endure increased second guessing from headquarters. For some there is the added stress of disrupting their family.

What of the journalism that they provide from the United States?

Part of it is equivalent to local news reporting. Neither Reuters nor the AP is going to tell the readers of *Goteborgs-Posten* about the Swedish chef who is the rage of New York. Fascination with how Korean companies are doing today on the New York Stock Exchange is limited outside Korea. Such home angles are underappreciated at news awards ceremonies, yet highly valued by consumers.

The United States, unlike many other places throughout the world, is not the site of bang-bang journalism, September 11, 2001, excepted. (Two young French filmmakers who happened to have been making a documentary about New York firefighters produced the only known video of the first plane striking Tower One.) Natalia Cruz remembers, "When the third building collapsed late in the afternoon, I was live. I was going to keep reporting, but police told me to run. I dropped my mike and said, 'I'm sorry. I've got to go,' on the air and started to run. My family was watching me on Telemundo International in Colombia. They were very worried." Yuri Kirilchenko of ITAR-TASS remembers, "I made four reports, eyewitness reports that the Russian media picked up from our wires. I think it was dusk when I felt extreme fatigue and a slight, dull pain in my chest. . . . They loaded me into an ambulance. . . . I was immediately diagnosed with a ruptured aorta. They said I had one hour to live if they didn't start treatment immediately. I was in major surgery for six hours."[7] Generally, however, the special skills of the war correspondent are not needed when reporting from America.

America, a vast and complex assignment, is a topic well suited for essayists. Big meals can be eaten in small helpings. In that regard, none surpassed Alistair Cooke, whose mellifluous voice delivered "Letter from America," fifteen minutes a week, on the BBC from 1946 until a month before his death in 2004. His British audience, Cooke told an interviewer, "tend to think of Americans as a people who are money mad, very ingenious, and take their food on the fly. It is the correspondent's job to startle those preconceptions. And sometimes, I admit, to say that they're right."[8] We found a modest number of stories in our "One Day" search that help to explain America—for example, a piece on Duke Ellington's 100th birthday for Brazilian television and the story about a high school prom for Dutch TV. We wish there had been more.

Rarely are foreign correspondents able to produce top-of-the-news material without "borrowing" news. We saw many stories that might as well have been translated and reprinted from the major U.S. media. It is hard to judge how much of the news about government is basically doctored translation. At least a third, we would guess, based on our "One Day" survey. That should not be surprising; what foreign news operation can match the resources of the Knight Ridder Washington bureau or the *Los Angeles Times*? And whatever the limitations of American journalism, it is safer to rely on it for the "facts" than on the journalism of any other country, as many of the foreign journalists noted in the "Context" chapter. Yet covering breaking news is how many in the foreign press corps in Washington are expected to spend their days, though the expectation is not as strong in New York or Los Angeles. Is such an allocation of resources based on journalistic judgment or organizational ego? Given the world trend to outsourcing, could foreign correspondence by translation not be done at headquarters or through wire services, thus releasing correspondents to do more of the sort of in-depth analysis that characterized their reporting in an earlier era? A distinguished Japanese journalist, after serving a tour in Washington, thinks, "The Japanese media take the easy way out, contenting themselves with homogeneous reporting and strangling the potential of the large numbers of reporters they send abroad."[9] At their best, foreign correspondents blend an insider's knowledge of their audience and their country's history with an outsider's insights into another country or culture.

The task we set for ourselves was to examine one element of "newswork" that had escaped serious attention and deserved exploration. Our questions were straightforward: Who are the foreign correspondents? How do they do their work? What do they report? Our purpose was not to advise the U.S. government on how to tell its story or spend its resources. Still, it should be undeniable that reaching out to foreign correspondents is a very good investment in the national interest.

Every day the Office of Research in the U.S. Department of State compiles "foreign media reactions," ten to twenty pages of extracts from news articles collected and translated by embassies around the world. The accounts by foreign correspondents in America are often critical of U.S. policies or politics,[10] but they do not have the vituperative edge, often veiled anti-Americanism, that originates in other places:

—"Had the United States not made so many enemies, innocent people might have been spared," *Guardian* (United Kingdom), regarding the 9/11 attacks.[11]

—"If one could encapsulate the essence of resentment toward the United States, it would have to be . . . their violent repression of those who don't serve America's global interests," *Daily Star* (Beirut).[12]

—"Both isolationist and controlling, it [the United States] is ignorant of the world it rules and oblivious to the suffering caused by many of its actions," *Mail and Guardian* (Johannesburg).[13]

Most journalistic images of the United States are produced by people who are not in the United States: editorialists, columnists, commentators, talk show hosts, headline writers, photo editors, and cartoonists in other countries. The place of foreign correspondents needs to be fitted into this context. Only foreign correspondents are given the opportunity to be there, to observe firsthand, to travel, to ask questions, and to report back on what they have discovered about another country. It is a unique job description—and of profound importance when the correspondents are reporting from a country that has a profound impact on the rest of the world.

A

Foreign Correspondents in the United States, by Place of Origin, 1964–2000

A ll information was taken from *Editor and Publisher International Year Book,* using back issues found in the Library of Congress. The 1971 and 1972 issues were missing; statistical averages were substituted in order to preserve the curve structure of the chart.

There are some fluctuations in the number of correspondents between years that suggest imperfections in the method used to compile the yearbook. That was especially true for Japanese correspondents. Previous research on this topic also suggests inconsistencies in compiling the data. The yearbook continued to list correspondents under the heading "Soviet Union" until 1995, only later listing them as citizens of Russia and other countries of the Commonwealth of Independent States. That was also the case with correspondents from the Czech Republic and Slovakia. We believe, however, that although the numbers for some countries had worrisome fluctuations, the tendencies in the regions tend to balance the fluctuations out, thereby illustrating accurate trends.

FIGURE A-1. Foreign Correspondents in the United States, by Place of Origin, 1964–2000

Number of correspondents

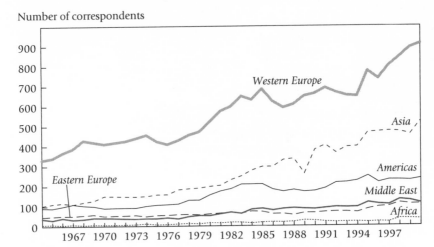

Source: *Editor and Publisher International Year Book,* various years.

Year	Eastern Europe	Western Europe	Asia	Middle East	Africa	Americas	Total
1964	46	331	103	37	7	92	616
1965	48	340	111	30	8	90	627
1966	51	366	116	40	5	99	677
1967	50	387	110	32	8	110	697
1968	54	429	120	35	5	103	746
1969	58	420	128	41	7	100	754
1970	50	411	150	40	6	90	747
1971	52	418	149	39	6	91	755
1972	53	425	148	37	7	92	762
1973	55	440	147	36	8	92	778
1974	49	456	150	38	12	101	806
1975	54	424	157	38	7	106	786
1976	55	409	158	42	8	108	780
1977	58	429	182	37	11	111	828
1978	59	456	187	48	13	130	893
1979	56	472	190	53	11	130	912
1980	61	522	198	52	16	156	1,005
1981	64	575	203	61	15	175	1,093
1982	68	598	231	69	19	186	1,171
1983	63	649	249	62	18	208	1,249
1984	73	631	277	83	14	208	1,286
1985	71	684	296	87	18	209	1,365
1986	60	623	296	78	20	183	1,260
1987	61	592	330	86	19	172	1,260
1988	54	608	336	89	21	180	1,288

FIGURE A-1. (*continued*)

Year	Eastern Europe	Western Europe	Asia	Middle East	Africa	Americas	Total
1989	65	649	261	86	28	171	1,260
1990	65	661	381	84	26	174	1,391
1991	69	691	404	89	21	188	1,462
1992	71	668	366	94	19	215	1,433
1993	70	652	394	92	20	217	1,445
1994	67	648	397	93	20	225	1,450
1995	84	775	467	116	18	249	1,709
1996	94	737	470	108	20	216	1,645
1997	97	801	474	105	19	229	1,725
1998	114	844	471	130	36	228	1,823
1999	107	891	457	125	35	226	1,841
2000	108	911	523	112	33	235	1,922

APPENDIX

B

Survey Questionnaire and Illustrative Responses

Our 1999 survey elicited responses from 439 foreign correspondents; we include here four completed questionnaires to illustrate the type of information that we received. Legibility was one criterion for inclusion. Too bad! Some of the most interesting responses were the most difficult to decipher. Confidentiality was not offered, yet we chose not to reproduce questionnaires that might complicate our respondents' relations with their employers.

Otherwise, we looked for as much diversity as is possible in a set of four. We included two correspondents based in Washington and two in New York; two men and two women; two from big countries (Japan and France) and two from small countries (Norway and New Zealand). One correspondent reported for a newspaper, one for radio, two for TV. They ranged in age from thirty-four to fifty-nine. One correspondent was American, two others had been students in the United States, the fourth worried about his fluency in English.

They were experienced journalists (from seven to twenty-six years in the business), who came to the United States from important jobs in their organizations (foreign editor, parliamentary correspondent, presenter), rather than from another foreign posting.

For the most part they covered hard news, such as "killer tornadoes" in Oklahoma or the East Timor Agreement at the United Nations, while on the lookout for a good feature, such as the opening of the movie *Star Wars*. Three of the four found regional stories to report in the week under study.

They indicated that reporting for other time zones complicated their newsgathering and made for a long workday. They complained of problems in reaching sources. They had different degrees of enthusiasm for the help offered by the Foreign Press Centers. They noted common stereotypes of Americans in their countries and indicated whether such perceptions affected their stories.

Brookings Institution
Foreign Correspondents Survey

Date: _05/21/1999_

Please print name: ___SABATIER   PATRICK.___

(Male)___ Female___ Age: _52_ Citizenship: _FRENCH.___

Place of birth: _FRANCE_____

News organization(s) you work for, list with country: ___LIBERATION (FRANCE)___

Permanent mailing address (where to send the book that will be based on the survey):

██████████████ WAHINGTON DC ██████████

Phone: ████████████████ E-mail ███████████

Please check which of the following descriptions best fits you:

X I am a journalist who has been sent here by my organization and will be reassigned after
 my tour of duty.
___ I am an American journalist employed by a non-American news organization.
___ I freelance for non-American news organizations.
___ None of the above. Explain:_____

Please check: My work is primarily for newspapers X ; for TV___ ; for magazines___ ;
for wire service___ ; for radio___ .

Do you do any non-journalism work? Yes X ; No___ ; if yes, describe: _Writing (essays &_
_fiction)_____ ; this takes _10_% of my time.

Please check: Foreign correspondence takes 100% of my time X ; half my time___ ; 25%___ ;
less than a day a week___ .

Number of years you have been a full-time journalist: _20_

Number of years in U.S. as foreign correspondent:____3____

(For non-Americans): Were you ever a student in the U.S.? (Yes)___ ; No___ ; if yes, describe
1 yr writing my thesis & giving French conversation classes at Suffolk U
(Boston)
What was your last post? (location, title, and dates) _Foreign Editor_____
____PARIS, 1992-1996_

2

Does your organization have a policy for how long it keeps correspondents in the U.S.?
No___; Yes _X_; if yes, number of years _4 to 8_

What do you think is the ideal number of years to be a foreign correspondent in the U.S.? _8_.
Why? _Lots to (dis)cover_

How many stories did you do in the last 7 days? _5_ Was this typical ___Yes _X_; No___;
if no, explain _____

How many of these stories were hard news? _2_ How many were features? _3_
How many of these stories mention your news organization's country or region? _1_ If any,
please describe _Interview with Stanley Karnow as his book Paris in_
the Fifties being published in France

What percent of your stories are suggested by your home office? _25_% What was the most
recent story your office wanted you to do? _Reactions in the US to Ehud_
Barak's election in Israel.

How do the stories your home office want differ from those you initiate? _Tend to be more_
linked to hard news.

How does your employer's time zone affect your work schedule? _makes it harder (_
dateline is about 2 p.m.)

In your news organization's country, what are common stereotypes of Americans and the
U.S.? _Arrogance, ignorance of rest of the world, money-centered_

Does this affect your stories in any way? _Need to be fought_

What stereotypes do you see in the U.S. media of your news organization's country?
Arrogance, anti-americanism, sense of cultural superiority

When were you last in the country where your news organization is located? _1 yr ago_

To what subjects or types of news should your organizations give more attention? _____
_____

Less attention? _____

List the U.S. cities where you spent an overnight on assignment in the last 12 months:
(1) _Denver_ (2) _Houston_ (3) _Philadelphia_
(4) _New York_ (5) _Orlando_ (6) _Chicago_
(7) _Atlanta_ (8) _Martha's Vineyard_ (9) _San Diego_
(10) _Los Angeles_ (11) _San Juan (Puerto Rico)_ (12) _____
Was this typical? _Yes._

3

Do you cover countries in addition to the U.S.? No (✓) ; Yes___; if yes, list countries you
visited last year:(1) _____(2) _____(3) _____
(4) _____(5) _____(6) _____
Was this typical?_____
Estimate the working days spent away from home last year: (0-7)___ (8-31)___
(32-60) X (61+)___

Correspondents for U.S. organizations sometimes find that spouses' work or having young
children limit the time they want to spend abroad. Are these considerations for you? No (✓) ,
Yes___; if yes, explain _____

Is English language fluency a concern to you? No (✓) ; Yes___; if yes, do you use
interpreters/translators? No___ Yes___.

How many free lance pieces did you do in 1998? ___.

What newspapers do you read daily? (List in order of importance to you)
NYTimes, WPost, WS Journal

What magazines do you read? Newsweek, Time, New Yorker, New Republic, Rolling Stone,
Wired, The Economist, People
What TV news programs do you watch? ABC World News, CNN

What radio do you listen to? NPR

How many hours (or minutes) do you spend online on the Internet on a typical workday? 2

How many work-related E-mail messages do you send on a typical day? 5

How many E-mail messages do you send to people outside the U.S. weekly? 20

Do you have a customized page online that gives you updates on specific news topics? Yes___
No (✓)

Do you regularly go online to check the headlines? Yes (✓) No___

Do you go online to read U.S. newspapers or magazines? Yes (✓) ; No___; if yes, which are
the most useful websites? USA Today, LA Times

Do you go online to get news of other countries? Yes (✓) ; No___; if yes, which are the most
useful websites? LIBERATION

4

Do you go online to do research? Yes◯___; No___; if yes, which websites do you use most frequently? *Yahoo, Excite,*

Of all the sources you have listed, from newspapers through online services, which is the most useful? *Newspapers*

Do you have problems reaching sources because you represent a non-U.S. news organizations? Yes◯___; No___; if yes, comment *There are always a hundred US news Organization ahead of you.*

How do you send your stories to your home office? *e-mail*

Do you use the U.S. government's Foreign Press Centers? Yes◯___ No___. If yes, on a scale of 1-5, with 5 being most useful to you, please rate each of these services: On-the-record briefings *3*; tours, such as to military bases *2*; help in arranging interviews *___*; office facilities, such as fax and magazines *___*; website information *3*. Are there other services that would be useful?

What do you find most frustrating about covering the U.S.? *So much - all the time*

What is most enjoyable about covering the U.S.? *— sauce on before*

What bothers you about the way your news organization covers the U.S.? (Please indicate if you want this to be confidential)

What could be done to improve coverage of the U.S.? *Have more correspondents*

What advice would you give to a correspondent coming to the U.S. for the first time? *Be ready to work a lot / don't get stuck in DC*

5

THE LAST QUESTIONS ARE ABOUT THE <u>MOST RECENT</u> STORY YOU HAVE COMPLETED.

What was the subject of the story?__Star War.__

How long was the story? (Words or seconds)__6000 signs.__

Where did you get the idea for this story? __All over the galaxy__

Describe preparing the story (using the following list):
      Star War fans

Events attended: (1) Convention in (2) _____ (3) _____
      Denver: the Star Was exhibit at the Smithsonian

Interviews: (1) Curator of the (2) _____ (3) _____

Documents: (1) Newspaper, magazine Thrise (2) _____ (3) _____

Other sources used: __Web sites__

Did you discuss the story with your home office before you did it? Yes ; No___; After you did it? Yes___ No___. Describe your home office's involvement in the story __None__

Was this story typical of your work? Yes ; No___; if no, explain: _____

WOULD IT BE POSSIBLE TO GET A COPY OF THIS STORY? Yes — enclosed

PLEASE SEND IT TO STEPHEN HESS, THE BROOKINGS INSTITUTION, 1775 MASSACHUSETTS AVE, NW, WASHINGTON, DC 20036; OR FAX: (202) 797-6144; OR E-MAIL: SHESS@BROOK.EDU.

Brookings Institution
Foreign Correspondents Survey

Date:_____

Please print name: ___HIROYUKI   ABE_____

Male ✓ Female___ Age: 43 Citizenship: __JAPAN____

Place of birth: __JAPAN_____

News organization(s) you work for, list with country: _____

FUJI   TELEVISION   NETWORK, Inc.   JAPAN_____

Permanent mailing address (where to send the book that will be based on the survey):

███

New York,   NY ███████████████████████

Phone: ████████████████_____E-mail ██████████████████████

Please check which of the following descriptions best fits you:

✓ I am a journalist who has been sent here by my organization and will be reassigned after
    my tour of duty.
___ I am an American journalist employed by a non-American news organization.
___ I freelance for non-American news organizations.
___ None of the above. Explain:_____

Please check: My work is primarily for newspapers___; for TV ✓; for magazines___;
for wire service___; for radio___.

Do you do any non-journalism work? Yes___; No ✓; if yes, describe: _____
_____; this takes ___% of my time.

Please check: Foreign correspondence takes 100% of my time ✓; half my time___; 25%___;
less than a day a week___.

Number of years you have been a full-time journalist: 7

Number of years in U.S. as foreign correspondent: 3

(For non-Americans): Were you ever a student in the U.S.? Yes___; No ✓; if yes, describe

_____

What was your last post? (location, title, and dates) Chief correspondent
in political news dept.

2

Does your organization have a policy for how long it keeps correspondents in the U.S.?
No _✓_ ; Yes___; if yes, number of years___

What do you think is the ideal number of years to be a foreign correspondent in the U.S.?___. _At least 3 years_
Why? _It takes at 3 to understand ✱ a different culture._

How many stories did you do in the last 7 days? _4_ Was this typical ___Yes _✓_ ; No___.;
if no, explain _____

How many of these stories were hard news? _3_ How many were features? _1_
How many of these stories mention your news organization's country or region? _1_ If any,
please describe _Prince & Princess Hitachinamiya in New York._

What percent of your stories are suggested by your home office? _80_ % What was the most
recent story your office wanted you to do? _Fuel Cell Electric cars._

How do the stories your home office want differ from those you initiate? _No difference._

How does your employer's time zone affect your work schedule? _Very much. It is hard to communicate._

In your news organization's country, what are common stereotypes of Americans and the
U.S.? _A lot of guns._

Does this affect your stories in any way? _Yes._

What stereotypes do you see in the U.S. media of your news organization's country?
Too much corruption.

When were you last in the country where your news organization is located? _Feb. 1999_

To what subjects or types of news should your organizations give more attention?_____
_____ _None in particular_ _____
Less attention? _____

List the U.S. cities where you spent an overnight on assignment in the last 12 months:
(1) _Detroit, MI_   (2) _Las Vegas, NV_ (3) _Richmond, VI_
(4) _Denver, CO_   (5) _San Antonio, TX_ (6) _Los Angeles, CA_
(7) _Salt Lake City, UT_ (8) _Leach Lake, MN_ (9) _Chicago, IL_
(10) _Houston, TX_   (11) _Chattanooga,_ (12) _St. Louis_
Was this typical? _yes_

3

Do you cover countries in addition to the U.S.? No___; Yes _✓_ ; if yes, list countries you
visited last year:(1) __Cuba__ (2) __Colombia__ (3) __Brasil__
(4) __Argentina__ (5) __Peru__ (6) __Honduras__
Was this typical? _Yes_ .
Estimate the working days spent away from home last year: (0-7)___ (8-31)___
(32-60)___ (61+) _✓_

Correspondents for U.S. organizations sometimes find that spouses' work or having young
children limit the time they want to spend abroad. Are these considerations for you? No _✓_,
Yes___; if yes, explain _____

Is English language fluency a concern to you? No___; Yes _✓_ ; if yes, do you use
interpreters/translators? No _✓_ Yes___ .

How many free lance pieces did you do in 1998? _0_ .

What newspapers do you read daily? (List in order of importance to you)
NY Times, Wall Street Journal

What magazines do you read? _Newsweek, Time_

What TV news programs do you watch? _News programs of CNN, ABC and NYI._

What radio do you listen to? _Anything_

How many hours (or minutes) do you spend online on the Internet on a typical workday? _2 hours_ .

How many work-related E-mail messages do you send on a typical day? _10_

How many E-mail messages do you send to people outside the U.S. weekly? _50_

Do you have a customized page online that gives you updates on specific news topics? Yes _✓_
No___

Do you regularly go online to check the headlines? Yes _✓_ No___

Do you go online to read U.S. newspapers or magazines? Yes _✓_; No___: if yes, which are
the most useful websites?_____
NY Times,

Do you go online to get news of other countries? Yes _✓_; No___; if yes, which are the most
useful websites?_____
CNN

4

Do you go online to do research? Yes _✓_; No___; if yes, which websites do you use most frequently?_____

CNN

Of all the sources you have listed, from newspapers through online services, which is the most useful? _All._

Do you have problems reaching sources because you represent a non-U.S. news organizations? Yes _✓_; No___; if yes, comment _____

PR people are impatient.   Takes time for a trivial request.

How do you send your stories to your home office? _Via e-mail, fax, Fedex, satelite_

Do you use the U.S. government's Foreign Press Centers? Yes _✓_ No___. If yes, on a scale of 1-5, with 5 being most useful to you, please rate each of these services: On-the-record briefings _2_; tours, such as to military bases _4_; help in arranging interviews _3_; office facilities, such as fax and magazines___; website information___. Are there other services that would be useful?_____

What do you find most frustrating about covering the U.S.?

Communicating.   (language problems)

What is most enjoyable about covering the U.S.?
being able to
Travel to all sorts of places.

What bothers you about the way your news organization covers the U.S.? (Please indicate if you want this to be confidential)   _None_

What could be done to improve coverage of the U.S.?

Improve English

What advice would you give to a correspondent coming to the U.S. for the first time?

Study English.

5

THE LAST QUESTIONS ARE ABOUT THE <u>MOST RECENT</u> STORY YOU HAVE
COMPLETED.

What was the subject of the story? _Fuel Cell Electric Cars_

How long was the story? (Words or seconds) _3 minutes 30 sec._

Where did you get the idea for this story? _From a my home country's magazine_

Describe preparing the story (using the following list):

Events attended: (1) _Test drives_ (2) _____ (3) _____

Interviews: (1) _GM_ (2) _Ford_ (3) _Daimler-Chrysler_

Documents: (1) _Press releases_ (2) _magazines_ (3) _web pages._

Other sources used: _Spoke with analysts_

Did you discuss the story with your home office before you did it? Yes _✓_; No___; After
you did it? Yes___ No___. Describe your home office's involvement in the story _____

We discussed the structure of the piece.

Was this story typical of your work? Yes _✓_; No___; if no, explain: _____

WOULD IT BE POSSIBLE TO GET A COPY OF THIS STORY? _It has not been aired yet. so unfortunately not at this time._

PLEASE SEND IT TO STEPHEN HESS, THE BROOKINGS INSTITUTION, 1775
MASSACHUSETTS AVE, NW, WASHINGTON, DC 20036; OR FAX: (202) 797-6144;
OR E-MAIL: SHESS@BROOK.EDU.

Brookings Institution
Foreign Correspondents Survey

Date: _5.7.99_

Please print name: _Christine Korme_

Male___ Female _X_ Age: _34_ Citizenship: _Norwegian_

Place of birth: _Oslo, Norway_

News organization(s) you work for, list with country: _TV2 Norway_

Permanent mailing address (where to send the book that will be based on the survey):

▌▌▌▌▌▌▌▌▌▌▌▌▌▌▌▌▌▌▌▌

Washington DC, ▌▌▌▌▌▌

Phone: ▌▌▌▌▌▌▌▌▌▌ E-mail ▌▌▌▌▌▌

Please check which of the following descriptions best fits you:

_X_ I am a journalist who has been sent here by my organization and will be reassigned after
my tour of duty.
___ I am an American journalist employed by a non-American news organization.
___ I freelance for non-American news organizations.
___ None of the above. Explain:_____

Please check: My work is primarily for newspapers___; for TV _X_; for magazines___;
for wire service___; for radio___.

Do you do any non-journalism work? Yes___; No _X_; if yes, describe: _____
_____; this takes ___% of my time.

Please check: Foreign correspondence takes 100% of my time _X_; half my time___; 25%___;
less than a day a week___.

Number of years you have been a full-time journalist: _13_

Number of years in U.S. as foreign correspondent: _1 1/2_

(For non-Americans): Were you ever a student in the U.S.? Yes _X_; No___; if yes, describe
BS Broadcasting, Syracuse University, NY, 1986

What was your last post? (location, title, and dates) _Political correspondent,_
Norwegian Parliment, News Anchor, News-room editor,
_TV2 — 1992 - 1998._

2

Does your organization have a policy for how long it keeps correspondents in the U.S.?
No____; Yes _X_ ; if yes, number of years _3-4_

What do you think is the ideal number of years to be a foreign correspondent in the U.S.? _3-5_
Why? _Shorter than 3 is too short, longer than 5 you could loose your sense of seeing things with "fresh" eyes._

How many stories did you do in the last 7 days? _4_ Was this typical _X_ Yes____; No____;
if no, explain _____

How many of these stories were hard news? _4_ How many were features? ____
How many of these stories mention your news organization's country or region? _O_ If any,
please describe_____

What percent of your stories are suggested by your home office? _20_% What was the most
recent story your office wanted you to do? _Oklahoma City tornado_

How do the stories your home office want differ from those you initiate? _We pretty much agree_

How does your employer's time zone affect your work schedule? _6 hour time difference between Norway and East Coast makes mornings frantic! The further West the worse it gets!_

In your news organization's country, what are common stereotypes of Americans and the
U.S.? _Loud mouthed, hamburger eating, less educated individuals. Everything is "big" in the US and slightly overdone._

Does this affect your stories in any way? _I try to show diversity!_

What stereotypes do you see in the U.S. media of your news organization's country?
The country of cold and snow, women's lib and clean air.

When were you last in the country where your news organization is located? _Christmas_

To what subjects or types of news should your organizations give more attention?_____
Foreign news
Less attention? _Human touch stories_

List the U.S. cities where you spent an overnight on assignment in the last 12 months:
(1) _Oklahoma City_   (2) _New York City_   (3) _Minneappolis_
(4) _Littleton/Denver_   (5) _LA_   (6) _Atlanta_
(7) _Miami_   (8) _New York City_   (9) _New York_
(10) _Orlando_   (11) _Orlando, NASA_   (12) _Jasper, Texas_
Was this typical? _No, would have travelled more. But impeachment made this year unique!_

3

Do you cover countries in addition to the U.S.? No___; Yes _X_; if yes, list countries you visited last year:(1) _Nicaragua_ (2) _Canada_ (3) _Mexico_
(4) _____ (5) _____ (6) _____
Was this typical? _Yes_
Estimate the working days spent away from home last year: (0-7)___ (8-31)___
(32-60) _※_ (61+) _X_

Correspondents for U.S. organizations sometimes find that spouses' work or having young children limit the time they want to spend abroad. Are these considerations for you? No _X_, Yes___; if yes, explain _____

Is English language fluency a concern to you? No _X_; Yes___; if yes, do you use interpreters/translators? No___ Yes___.

How many free lance pieces did you do in 1998? _O_.

What newspapers do you read daily? (List in order of importance to you)
NY Times, Washington Post, USA Today

What magazines do you read? _Newsweek, Time, The Economist_

What TV news programs do you watch? _Just about everything!_

What radio do you listen to? _NPR, CBS_

How many hours (or minutes) do you spend online on the Internet on a typical workday? _1-2_

How many work-related E-mail messages do you send on a typical day? _5_

How many E-mail messages do you send to people outside the U.S. weekly? _10-15_

Do you have a customized page online that gives you updates on specific news topics? Yes___ No _X_

Do you regularly go online to check the headlines? Yes _X_ No___

Do you go online to read U.S. newspapers or magazines? Yes _X_; No___; if yes, which are the most useful websites? _Newslinks_

Do you go online to get news of other countries? Yes _X_; No___; if yes, which are the most useful websites? _Local newspapers in countries/cities you are travelling to, and Norwegian papers._

4

Do you go online to do research? Yes _X_ ; No___; if yes, which websites do you use most frequently? _Local Papers/ TV stations_

Of all the sources you have listed, from newspapers through online services. which is the most useful? _NY Times, CNN, Washington Post, Reuters_

Do you have problems reaching sources because you represent a non-U.S. news organizations? Yes _X_ ; No___; if yes, comment _This is THE BIGGEST problem in the US! ~~By~~ ~~Rep It~~ officials don't get on TV in the States, they just don't bother. DC is the worst in that sense!_

How do you send your stories to your home office? _Satellite/ ISDN phone lines._

Do you use the U.S. government's Foreign Press Centers? Yes _X_ No___. If yes, on a scale of 1-5, with 5 being most useful to you, please rate each of these services: On-the-record briefings _3_ ; tours, such as to military bases _1_ ; help in arranging interviews _4_ ; office facilities, such as fax and magazines _4_ ; website information _5_. Are there other services that would be useful?_____

What do you find most frustrating about covering the U.S.? _To get interviews with officials, politicians etc. PR outside of the US is not regarded as PR, now matter how big your station is!_

What is most enjoyable about covering the U.S.? _Great country, nice people — the average American on the street loves to be on TV (!) — a very diverse country._

What bothers you about the way your news organization covers the U.S.? (Please indicate if you want this to be confidential) _Well, since I do the coverage — nothing, really._

What could be done to improve coverage of the U.S.? _To hire a producer to do research._

What advice would you give to a correspondent coming to the U.S. for the first time? _Get outside the Beltway!_

---

* _With the exception of some institutions like American University, Brookings and Cato. Believe me, we are very greatful !_

5

THE LAST QUESTIONS ARE ABOUT THE <u>MOST RECENT</u> STORY YOU HAVE COMPLETED.

What was the subject of the story? _Killer tornado Oklahoma City_

How long was the story? (Words or seconds) _2:16 + a live shot._

Where did you get the idea for this story? _CNN_

Describe preparing the story (using the following list):

Events attended: (1)_____ (2) _____ (3) _____

Interviews: (1)_____ (2) _____ (3) _____

Documents: (1)_____ (2) _____ (3) _____

If you call this preparation:
~~Other sources used:~~ _- "The death toll is rising - should I go?"_
- "Yes".

Did you discuss the story with your home office before you did it? Yes_X_; No___; After you did it? Yes___ No_X_. Describe your home office's involvement in the story _____

They booked the live shot from Oklahoma, briefed me on wirenews

Was this story typical of your work? Yes___; No___; if no, explain: _It's typical_

for a hard news breaking story.

WOULD IT BE POSSIBLE TO GET A COPY OF THIS STORY? _Yes, call me if you want it._

PLEASE SEND IT TO STEPHEN HESS, THE BROOKINGS INSTITUTION, 1775 MASSACHUSETTS AVE, NW, WASHINGTON, DC 20036; OR FAX: (202) 797-6144; OR E-MAIL: SHESS@BROOK.EDU.

Brookings Institution
Foreign Correspondents Survey

Date: _MAY 13 1999_

Please print name: _JUDY LESSING_

Male___ Female _✓_ Age: _59_ Citizenship: _US / NEW ZEALAND_

Place of birth: _AUCKLAND, NEW ZEALAND_

News organization(s) you work for, list with country: _RADIO NEW ZEALAND,_
NEW ZEALAND

Permanent mailing address (where to send the book that will be based on the survey):

_▓▓▓▓▓▓▓▓▓▓▓▓▓▓▓_

BROOKLYN NY ▓▓▓▓▓

Phone: _▓▓▓▓▓▓▓▓▓_   E-mail _▓▓▓▓▓▓▓▓▓▓▓_

Please check which of the following descriptions best fits you:

____ I am a journalist who has been sent here by my organization and will be reassigned after
     my tour of duty.
_✓_ I am an American journalist employed by a non-American news organization.
____ I freelance for non-American news organizations.
____ None of the above. Explain:_____

Please check: My work is primarily for newspapers___; for TV___; for magazines___;
for wire service___; for radio _✓_ .

Do you do any non-journalism work? Yes___; No _✓_; if yes, describe: _____
_____ ; this takes ___% of my time.

Please check: Foreign correspondence takes 100% of my time _✓_; half my time___; 25%___;
less than a day a week___.

Number of years you have been a full-time journalist: _26_

Number of years in U.S. as foreign correspondent: _24_

(For non-Americans): Were you ever a student in the U.S.? Yes___; No___; if yes, describe
_____

What was your last post? (location, title, and dates) _WITH RADIO NEW ZEALAND NEWS_
SINCE 1975. PREVIOUSLY A PRESENTER AT RADIO NEW ZEALAND
_1961-64, 1965-71._

2

Does your organization have a policy for how long it keeps correspondents in the U.S.?
No _✓_; Yes___; if yes, number of years___

What do you think is the ideal number of years to be a foreign correspondent in the U.S.? _5 minimum_
Why? _A COMPLEX COUNTRY TAKES TIME TO BE ABSORBED, UNDERSTOOD_

How many stories did you do in the last 7 days? _21_ Was this typical ___Yes _✓_; No___;
if no, explain _SLIGHTLY BELOW AVERAGE - KOSOVO WAR TAKES SPACE USUALLY OCCUPIED BY US & UNITED NATIONS STORIES_
How many of these stories were hard news? _16_ How many were features? _5_
How many of these stories mention your news organization's country or region? _6_ If any,
please describe _EAST TIMOR AGREEMENT IS AN IMPORTANT REGIONAL STORY_

What percent of your stories are suggested by your home office? _20_% What was the most
recent story your office wanted you to do? _EAST TIMOR; KOSOVO REFUGEES (EQUAL WEIGHT)_

How do the stories your home office want differ from those you initiate? _THEY USUALLY DON'T DIFFER IN SUBJECT BUT CAN IN FREQUENCY_

How does your employer's time zone affect your work schedule? _YES. N.Z IS 16 HOURS AHEAD, SO BULK OF STORIES FILED ARE IN AFTERNOON & EVENING, BUT GATHERING THEM BEGINS IN MY MORNING — THAT IS, LONG WORK HOURS_
In your news organization's country, what are common stereotypes of Americans and the
U.S.? _THAT AMERICANS HAVE MORE DISPOSABLE INCOME; SOCIETY HERE IS PRONE TO VIOLENCE; THAT AMERICANS GO TO COURT TO SETTLE SOCIAL ISSUES_

Does this affect your stories in any way? _SOMEWHAT_

What stereotypes do you see in the U.S. media of your news organization's country?
NEW ZEALAND RARELY APPEARS IN US MEDIA WHICH I MONITOR

When were you last in the country where your news organization is located? _NOV. 1997_

To what subjects or types of news should your organizations give more attention? _SOCIAL TRENDS WHICH AFFECT AMERICAN THINKING_
Less attention? _SUDDEN CATASTROPHES WITHOUT LASTING IMPACT; # POLICE & AMBULANCE CHASING_
List the U.S. cities where you spent an overnight on assignment in the last 12 months:
(1) _WASHINGTON_   (2) _MILWAUKEE_   (3) _BOSTON_
(4) _MILWAUKEE_   (5) _____   (6) _____
(7) _____   (8) _____   (9) _____
(10) _____   (11) _____   (12) _____
Was this typical? _YES_

3

Do you cover countries in addition to the U.S.? No ✓; Yes___; if yes, list countries you visited last year:(1) _____(2) _____(3) _____
(4) _____(5) _____(6) _____
Was this typical?_____
Estimate the working days spent away from home last year: (0-7)___ (8-31) ✓
(32-60)___ (61+)___

Correspondents for U.S. organizations sometimes find that spouses' work or having young children limit the time they want to spend abroad. Are these considerations for you? No ✓,
Yes___; if yes, explain _____

Is English language fluency a concern to you? No ✓; Yes___; if yes, do you use interpreters/translators? No___ Yes___.

How many free lance pieces did you do in 1998? 7 .

What newspapers do you read daily? (List in order of importance to you)
NEW YORK TIMES _____

What magazines do you read? THE NEW YOAKER. THE NATION. BROOKLYN BRIDGE

What TV news programs do you watch? PBS NEWSHOUR; SOME CNN _____

What radio do you listen to? WCBS NEWS RADIO; WNYC - NPR PRI STATION

How many hours (or minutes) do you spend online on the Internet on a typical workday? 1

How many work-related E-mail messages do you send on a typical day? 4

How many E-mail messages do you send to people outside the U.S. weekly? 12

Do you have a customized page online that gives you updates on specific news topics? Yes___
No ✓

Do you regularly go online to check the headlines? Yes ✓ No___

Do you go online to read U.S. newspapers or magazines? Yes ✓; No___; if yes, which are the most useful websites? SLATE.COM _____

_____

Do you go online to get news of other countries? Yes ✓; No___; if yes, which are the most useful websites? NEWSROOM.CO.NZ   BBC.CO.UK _____

_____

4

Do you go online to do research? Yes___; No _✓_; if yes, which websites do you use most frequently?_____

_____

Of all the sources you have listed, from newspapers through online services, which is the most useful? _NEWSPAPERS — BUT NPR NEWS IS EVEN BETTER_____

Do you have problems reaching sources because you represent a non-U.S. news organizations? Yes _✓_; No___; if yes, comment _HARD TO GET CALLS RETURNED; NEW___

_ZEALAND IS NOT CONSIDERED IMPORTANT ENOUGH FOR MOST OFFICES,___
GROUPS — N.Y. CITY HALL, THE WHITE HOUSE & PUBLISHERS ARE WORST
How do you send your stories to your home office? _PHONE_____

Do you use the U.S. government's Foreign Press Centers? Yes _✓_ No___. If yes, on a scale of 1-5, with 5 being most useful to you, please rate each of these services: On-the-record briefings _3_; tours, such as to military bases _4_; help in arranging interviews _1_; office facilities, such as fax and magazines _—_; website information _2_. Are there other services that would be useful? _PROBABLY NOT, THOUGH DECENT AUDIO FEEDS AT___

BROADCAST QUALITY FROM WASHINGTON BRIEFINGS INTO NYFPC WOULD BE NICE.

What do you find most frustrating about covering the U.S.?
THE AMERICAN MEDIA'S TAKE ON US IMPORTANCE, THE ACCEPTANCE OF

_U.S. SPIN BY MY EDITORS_____

What is most enjoyable about covering the U.S.?
_VARIETY OF TOPICS_____

_____

What bothers you about the way your news organization covers the U.S.? (Please indicate if you want this to be confidential)
ITS LACK OF FINANCIAL RESOURCES PREVENTS PROPER TRAVEL; ITS 24 HOUR
NEWS CYCLE MAKES WORK ON FEATURES DIFFICULT; SOME EDITORS
WANT INSTANT NEWS WHICH LEADS TO SUPERFICIAL COVERAGE

What could be done to improve coverage of the U.S.?
_FIX ALL OF THE ABOVE_____

_____

What advice would you give to a correspondent coming to the U.S. for the first time?
_READ AS MUCH FICTION AS YOU CAN; TRY NOT TO BRING_____

STEREOTYPICAL THINKING WITH YOU; BE OPEN TO IDEAS, EVENTS,

BUT DON'T LOSE YOUR ABILITY TO THINK FOR YOURSELF

5

THE LAST QUESTIONS ARE ABOUT THE <u>MOST RECENT</u> STORY YOU HAVE COMPLETED.

What was the subject of the story? _KOSOUO   REFUGEES AT FORT DIX_

How long was the story? (Words or seconds) _3' 44"_

Where did you get the idea for this story? _OWN IDEA; HELPED BY FPC ARRANGING GROUP ACCESS_

Describe preparing the story (using the following list):

Events attended: (1) _2_____ (2) _____ (3) _____

Interviews: (1) _MULTIPLE_____ (2) _____ (3) _____

Documents: (1) _NEWS ACCOUNTS_ (2) _____ (3) _____

Other sources used: _____

Did you discuss the story with your home office before you did it? Yes _✓_; No___; After you did it? Yes___ No _✓_. Describe your home office's involvement in the story _EDITOR_

_LIKED IDEA, SAID GO FOR IT_____

Was this story typical of your work? Yes _✓_; No___; if no, explain: _____

_____

WOULD IT BE POSSIBLE TO GET A COPY OF THIS STORY? _ATTACHED — NOT FOR RE BROADCAST_

PLEASE SEND IT TO STEPHEN HESS, THE BROOKINGS INSTITUTION, 1775 MASSACHUSETTS AVE, NW, WASHINGTON, DC 20036; OR FAX: (202) 797-6144; OR E-MAIL: SHESS@BROOK.EDU.

Respondents, Surveys, and Interviews

Note: Asterisk indicates an interview; some interviewees also responded to our surveys.

Algeria

Mouny Berrah

Argentina

Jacqueline Aidenbaum
Ana Barow
Monica Flores-Correa
Marina Gilbert
*Edgardo Carlos Krebs
Maria O'Donnell

Armenia

*David Zenian

Australia

*Jeff Barker
Peter Curtis
*Joanne Gray
Brian Hale
*Tim Lester
*Jeff McMullen
Craig McMurtrie
Dale Paget
Robert Penfold
*Mark Riley
*Jim Rosenberg
Cameron Stewart
Michelle Stone
*Bruce Wilson

Austria

Peter Fritz
*Eugen A. Freund

Bettina M. Gordon
Susanne Newrkla
*Annabel Pigerstorfer
*Monica Riedler

Belgium

Yve J. Laudy
Nathalie Mattheiem
*Thomas Ronse

Bosnia and Herzegovina

*Envera Selimovic

Brazil

Ricardo Bairos
*Getulio Bittencourt
Heloisa Maria Villela De Castro
Chris Delboni
Danielle Machado Duran
Jennifer Gonzales
*Roberto Gracia
Lucia Guimaraes
Herbert Henning
Lucas Mendes
Jose M. Passos
David Presas
Flavia Sekles
*Carlos Lins da Silva
*Fernando Silvo-Pinto
*Paulo Sotero
Angelica F. Vieira

Bulgaria

Linoor Fortunove-Russell

Canada

Jeffrey Allan
*Henry Champ
Andrew Cohen
Yvette Czigli
Frank Koller
*Alan Fryer
Guy Gendron
David Halton
*Carl Hanlon
Patrick Harden
Richard Hetu
Kathleen Kenna
*Barry McKenna
*Brian Milner
Helene Y. Parenteau
*Mike Shea
*Mark Sikstrom
Frank Valler
Jennifer Westaway

Chile

*Lydia Bendersky

China

Curtis C. Cutter
*Yan Feng
Zhenqiu Gu
Zhengxin Li
Shaowen Lin
Mumin Rong
*Rujun Wang
*Wei Tian
Xiaoyang Xia
*Meihua Xie
Lei Yang

Colombia

*Andres Cavelier
Sergio Gomez
Elizabeth Mora-Mass
*Marcela Sanchez

Croatia

Fjodor Polojac

Cyprus

*Michalis Ignatiou

Czech Republic

Petra Flanderkova
*Josef Schrabel

Denmark

Tom Buk-Swienty
Torsten Jansen
Jannich Kofoed
Lotte Lund Eriksen
Sven Rye
Michael Ulveman

Egypt

*Adib Andrawis
*Mahfouz Doss
Mohamed Elsetouhi
Khaled Mansour
*Mohamed ElSayed Said

Finland

Mikael Crawford
Tomi Ervamaa
Eeva Haltsonen
Erkki Kanto
Ilona Kanto
Reijo Lindroos
Laura Pekonen
Paivi Sinisalo
Matti Torma

France

Jacqueline Albert-Simon
Catherine Antoine
Patrice de Beer
Cecile Besson
Philippe Boulet-Gercourt
Jean-Bernard Cadier
Stephanie Chayet
Romain Clergeat
Martine Combemale
Karine Cohen
Caroline Crosdale
Dominique Derda
*Christophe de Roquefeuil
Jean-Louis Doublet
Christiana Fabiani
Jerome Godefroy

Ulysse Gosset
Laura Haim
Nathaniel Harrison
*Olivier Knox
Camille Labro
Michael Langan
Gaetan Lecointe
M. David Levin
Karen Leslie Lowe
Henriette Lowisch
Michele Mattei
*Jean-Jaques Mevel
Olivier Pascal
Philippe Reltien
*Patrick Sabatier
Gilles Senges
Yvan Trousselle

Germany

*Jim Anderson
Karin Assmann
Udo L. Bauer
Michael Baumann
Elmar Biebl
*Tom Buhrow
Herta Borniger
Siegfried Buschschlueter
Doris Chevron
Agostino Della Porta
Laura Downhower
*Stefan W. Elfenbein
Martin Ganslmeier
Silke Gondolf
Peter Gruber
Klaus Jurgen Haller
Martin Halusa
Matthias Held
Ralf Hoogestraat
Roger Horne
Gertrud A. Hussla
Georg O. Kellermann
*Claus Kleber
Konstantin Klein
Thomas Knipp
Stefan Kornelius
Deborah Kraus
Christof Lang
*Rudiger Lentz
Rainer Lindberg
Verena Leuken
*Christina Maier

Karen Martin
Michele Mattei
*Annette Moll
*Siri Nyrop
*Sabine Reifenberg
Marianne Schaefer-Trench
Holger Schmale
Gunnar J. Schultz-Burkel
Rainer Stadler
*Peter Tautfest
Christian Tenbrock
Thomas Unipp
Alexander von Wechmar
Clemens Verenkotte
*Helmut Voss
Leo Wieland
Martin Winter
Uwe Wolff
*Dietrich Zwaetz

Greece

*Dimitris Y. Apokis
*Thomas Ellis
*Michalis Ignatiou
Panagiotis Papadopoulos
John Perdikis
Dina Pinos

Guatemala

Cesar A. Orantes

Honduras

*Jacobo Goldstein

Hong Kong

Lotus Chau
Siu Wai Cheung
Dodi Fromson
Charlotte Rong Li
*Charles A. Snyder

Hungary

*Andras Heltai
*Janos Karpati
Agnes Niemetz
Zita Vilmanyi

Iceland

*Helga Petuksson

India

*Ramesh Chandran
*Ashok Easwaran
Munish Gupta
Sridhar Krishnaswami
*Nambalat C. Menon
Innaiah Narisetti
*T. V. Parasuram
Raj S. Rangarajan
Probir Kumar Sarkar

Indonesia

Akhmad Kusaeni
Irawan Nugroho
*Hidajat S. Supangkat

Ireland

Susan Falvella-Garraty
*Mark Little
*John O'Mahony
*Patrick Smyth

Iraq

Malih Salih Shukur

Israel

*Dovik Ashdot
*Jonathan Broder
Marilyn Henry
*Hillel Kuttler
Benjamin Landau
*Tom Tugend
*Janine Zacharia

Italy

Francesco Luigi Bonazzi
Franco Borrelli
Giuseppe Buscemi
Mauro Calamandrei
Antonio Carlucci
*Ennino Carreto
Luca Celada

Christiano Del Riccio
Luca Dini
Andrea Fiano
Massimo Jaus
Elisa Leonelli
Massimo Lopes Pegna
Paolo Longo
*Stefano Marchi
Paolo Mastrolilli
Marino de Medici
Marco Moretti
Gastone Orefice
Franco Pantarelli
Piero Piccardi
*Giampaolo Pioli
*Gianna Pontecorboli
Gabriele Romagnoli
Stefano Trincia
Andrew Visconti
Arturo Zampaglione

Japan

Hiroyuki Abe
Masaaki Aoki
Momoe Ban
Narra Briscoe
Kanako Chiba
Megan Devir
*Peter Ennis
Paul E. Flatin
*Yuko Fuse
Takaji Hamashima
John B. Hanshaw
Shin Hara
Masaaki Harukawa
Atushi Hatayama
*Mike Hayashi
Yoko Hirasawa
*Masahiko Hisae
Masao Hosoda
Yoshio Hotta
Yoshiyuki Itsumi
Hiroshi Kanashige
Maho Kawachi
Koji Kawamura
*Shigeru Komago
*Lisa Lane
Tetsu Machida
*Toshiyuki Matsuyama
Takaaki Mizuno
Shinichi Murakami

Shin-ichiro Muraoka
*Yasuhisa Nakada
Yoshio Ninosiki
*Norimichi Okai
*Noboru Okamoto
Hitoshi Omae
*Hideko Otake
Abigail H. Regier
Kunio Saijo
*Nobuyoshi Sakajiri
Shinichiro Sakikawa
*Atsushi Sato
Shigebumi Sato
Shiro Segawa
Katsuyoshi Seimiya
Takashi Settai
Toru Shiba
Osamu Sorimachi
Yoshiko Sugimoto
Hiroki Sugita
*Mary Ellen Swift
Hitoshi Suzuki
Kyoko Suzuki
*Akio Takahata
Toru Takanarita
Shuichi Tomaru
Tadao Uchida
Aiko Yabuki
Tsutomu Yamaguchi
Akira Yamamoto
Nami Yamamoto
*Takeshi Yamashita
Kazutami Yamazaki
Naofumi Yoshiike

Jordan

*Mohammad Al-Dakamseh

Korea

You Yeon Chae
*Soon-Whan Cho
Guem Nak Choe
*Chang Young Choi
Chul-Ho Choi
Wang Sok Eom
*Yong-Joong Joo
Jeong-Woo Kil
Inyoung Kim
B. J. Yang

Kuwait

*Adnan Aljadi
Faisal S. Alzaid
James C. Flanigan
Wafik Ramadan

Lebanon

Samir F. Karam
Samir N. Nader

Lithuania

Gintautas Alksninis

Macedonia

Lilica Kitanovska

Mali

*Adam Ououloguem

Mauritius

*Pamela Glass

Mexico

Ricardo Alday
Gerardo Cardenas
*Jose Carreno
*Jesus P. Esquivel
Dolia Estevez
Maria Isabel Gonzalez
*Philip Klint
Cesar Romero
*Yolanda Sanchez
Alejandra Villasmil
Naief Yehya

Netherlands

Juurd Eijsvoogel
*Charles Groenhuijsen
Benno Groeneveld
David H. Hammelburg
Theo Kingma
Bert Lanting
Monique Martens
Tim Overdiek

Freke Vuijst
John B. Wanders
Max Westerman

New Zealand

*Judy Lessing

Nigeria

*Jerome Hule

Norway

Alf B. Johnsen
Christine Korme
Helge Ogrim
Finne Thurmann-Nielsen

Pakistan

Asif Raja

Panama

*Betty Brannan Jaen
*Oswaldo Valenzuela

Philippines

Jennie L. Ilustre

Poland

Pawel Burdzy
Wieslaw Cyprys
Tomasz Deptula
*Max Kolonko
Jan Palarczyk
Agnieszka Pukniel
Violetta Slodzinka
*Marek Tomaszewski
Bartosz Weglarczyk
*Tomasz Zalewski

Portugal

Luis Costa Ribas
Rui Coimbra
Manuel Ricardo Ferreira
Carlos Fino

Anthony Jenkins
*Theresa Lobo
Luis M. Pires
Luis Ribas
Barbara Reis

Romania

*Ray Arco
Gabriel Plesea
Bianca Popescu

Russia

Yuri Kirilchenko
Victor Logachev
*Andrei K. Sitov
Vladimir Sukhoi
*Nickolay Zimin

Saudi Arabia

Tom Canahuate
Dean Dessouky
*Susan Gray
Mohamed El-Maddah
*Barbara G. B. Ferguson
Tim Kennedy
Mohammad Salih

Senegal

Aly K. Ndaw
*Ibru Wane

Singapore

*Lee Siew Hua

Slovakia

*Olga Bakova
Ivo Kunsch
Julia Ondrejcekova

South Africa

*Hannes De Wet
*Johann A. Holzapfel
Jeffrey Morrissey
*Pierre Steyn

Spain

*Jorge A. Banales
Rafael Canas
Juan Cavestany
Javier Del Pino
Albert Guasch
Alberto Garcia Marrder
Xavier Mas de Xaxas
Francisco Medina
Jaime Meilan
Isabel Piquer
Agustin Remesal
*Pedro J. Rodriguez
Barbara Probst Solomon
Montserrat Vendrell

Sudan

Mohannad Salih

Sweden

Lars Adaktusson
Lena Almstrom
Gunilla Faringer
*Karin Henriksson
Kurt Malarstedt
Cecilia Udden Mannheimer
Ulf Martensson
*Lars Moberg
Morgan Olofsson
Hans Inge Olsson
Nicole O'Neill
*Lennart Pehrson

Switzerland

Roberto Antonini
Mario Casella
Michelle Karen
Bernard Rappaz
Casper M. Selg
Peter Schibli
Marlene von Arx

Taiwan

Benjamin Suo-pong Chang
Stacy B. J. Chao
Jay Chen
Ava Chien

Nelson Chung
*Norman Fu
Jennifer J. Huang
Ernie Ko
Kuanyuh Tony Lin
Herman Y. C. Pan
*Louise Ran
Anni Shih
Erich Shih
Nadia Y. F. Tsao

Thailand

Charles Ellis

Turkey

Asli Aydintasbas
*Yasemin Congar
*Yucel Donmez
Harun Kazaz
Garbis Kesisoglu
Savas Suzal
Ender Ulgen
*Dogan Uluc

United Arab Emirates

Fouzi El-Asmar
Leo Scanlon

United Kingdom

Zanny Minton Beddoes
Jeffrey Blyth
Daniel Bogler
*Julian Borger
*Henry Brandon
Louise Branson
Ian Brodie
Patrick Brogan
Carol S. Castiel
Lauren Chambliss
Tom Carver
Mary Dejevsky
*Gabrielle Donnelly
Stephen Fidler
*Toby Harnden
John Hiscock
Bridget Kendall
Martin Kettle
Richard Lister

*William Lowther
*Barbara McMahon
Andrew R. Marshall
John Micklethwait
*John Parker
Christopher Reed
Gregory Robb
*Andrew Roy
Sue Russell
Charles Seife
David A. Smith
Norberto Svarzman
Philippa Thomas
*Nikki Tait
David Wastell
Charles Wheelan
Richard Wolffe

Uruguay

*Marco Maggi

Venezuela

Everett A. Bauman
Aida Raygada

Yugoslavia

Mira Panajotovic
*Dubravka Savic

Multiple Countries

Hugues-Denver Akassy
*Hafez Al-Mirazi

Philip Berk
Ihsan Bouabid
Jenny Cooney Carrillo
Ivor Davis
Jose A. Delgado
Raghida Dergham
Nick Douglas
Maureen Dragone
Thabet El Bardicy
Gaetana Enders
*Abderrahim Foukara
Sabine Guez
Algirdas Gustaitis
*George Hishmeh
*Russell Warren Howe
William Kao-Dor Loh
Danielle Knight
Uwe Knupfer
*Ronald Krueger
Ahmed Lateef
*Connie Lawn
Lucas Ligtenberg
Jim Lobe
*Simon Marks
Mitchell Martin
*Lawrie Mastersonn
Khalil Matar
Maria Elena Matheus-Atchley
Tony Perrottet
*Claude Porsella
Hans Sandberg
Lisa Sandberg
Norberto Svarzman
Jacques Tiziou
Charlie Torrini
*Ian Williams

Notes

GUIDE

1. For example, see Bill Lawrence, *Six Presidents, Too Many Wars* (Saturday Review Press, 1972). Lawrence covered the White House for the *New York Times* and ABC. He writes: "I came to know all these men [presidents Franklin Roosevelt through Richard Nixon] well, well enough so each of them called me 'Bill' " (p. 6).

2. Leo C. Rosten's Ph.D. dissertation from the University of Chicago, published as *The Washington Correspondents* (1937; repr. Arno Press, 1974).

3. Dan D. Nimmo, *Newsgathering in Washington: A Study in Political Communication* (New York: Atherton, 1964).

4. Bernard G. Cohen, *The Press and Foreign Policy* (Princeton University Press, 1963).

5. The Newswork series and the following books, which I wrote or edited during this period, were published by the Brookings Institution Press: *The Presidential Campaign* (1974, 1978, 1988), *Organizing the Presidency* (1976, 1988, 2002), *Presidents and the Presidency* (1996), *News and Newsmaking* (1996), *The Little Book of Campaign Etiquette* (1998, 2002), and *The Media and the War on Terrorism* (2003), with Marvin Kalb. I also contributed chapters to the Brookings books *Elections American Style* (1987), *Critical Choices* (1989), *Congress, the Press, and the Public* (1994), *The Permanent Campaign and Its Future* (2000), *Innocent until Nominated* (2001), and *United We Serve* (2003); and to *Media Power: Professionals and Policies* (Routledge, 2000) and, with Kathryn Dunn Tenpas, to *Considering the Bush Presidency* (Oxford, 2004).

6. On the "Image of the United States," the report concludes, "When the publics of the 16 nations covered by the survey were asked to give favorability ratings of five major leading nations—the United States, Germany, China, Japan, and France—the U.S. fared the worst of the group." On the "Image of the American people," the conclusion was that "the favorability ratings of Americans have declined since 2002 in 9 of the 12 countries for which data exists for that year." The Pew Global Attitudes Project, June 23, 2005, pp. 1, 2, 11, and 20. However, as Anne Applebaum points out, there are still people in the world who admire Americans. See her "In Search of Pro-Americanism," *Foreign Policy* (July-August 2005): 32–40.

7. U.S. Department of State, remarks of Secretary Condoleezza Rice, March 14, 2005.

8. See Patrick Bishop, "America's Hard Cash and Soft Words Fail to Woo Arabs," *Daily Telegraph* (London), March 25, 2005; Corey Pein, "The New Wave," *Columbia Journalism Review* (May–June 2005): 28; and Neil King Jr., "Sparking Debate, Radio Czar Retools Government Media," *Wall Street Journal*, June 20, 2005.

9. See Paul Singer, "But Did the CIA Kill Kennedy?" *National Journal*, June 4, 2005, p. 1694; see also the Department of State web page: http://usinfo.state.gov/media/media_resources/misinformation.html.

10. Lars Willnat and David Weaver, "Through Their Eyes: The Work of Foreign Correspondents in the United States," *Journalism* 4, no. 4 (2003): 403–04. Also see Stephen Hess and Marvin Kalb, *The Media and the War on Terrorism*, chapters on foreign correspondents, pp. 198–219, and public diplomacy, pp. 223–86.

11. Facsimiles of completed questionnaires and a list of survey and interview respondents can be found in the appendixes.

12. Jeremy Tunstall, *The Media Are American* (Columbia University Press, 1977).

CONTEXT

1. "Foreign Correspondent Reflects on Reporting in Iraq," *Centerpoint*, September 2004 (Woodrow Wilson International Center for Scholars newsletter).

2. Excellent introductions to this subject include Robert L. Stevenson, *Global Communication in the Twenty-First Century* (Longman, 1994), and Melvin L. DeFleur and Everette E. Dennis, *Understanding Mass Communication* (Houghton Mifflin, 2002).

3. See Jon Vanden Heuvel and Everette E. Dennis, *The Unfolding Lotus: East Asia's Changing Media* (Freedom Forum Media Studies Center, 1993).

4. See John C. Merrill, "Global Media: A Newspaper Community of Reason," *Media Studies Journal* 4 (Fall 1990): 93.

5. Anne Nelson's students are listed by country in the acknowledgments, as are the diplomats who were interviewed by the Brookings interns in Washington.

6. See Adrian Karatnycky, "The 2003 Freedom House Survey: National Income and Liberty," *Journal of Democracy* 15 (January 2004): 82–93.

7. Quoted in George Kennedy, "The British See Things Differently," *Columbia Journalism Review* (March/April 2002), p. 49.

8. Bill Kovach and Tom Rosenstiel, *Warp Speed: America in the Age of Mixed Media* (Century Foundation Press, 1999), p. 9.

9. Norway, Sweden, Denmark, Finland, and Iceland, with a combined population of 20 million, had forty-three correspondents listed in the State Department's 2002 directory. In contrast, China, population 1.3 billion, listed thirty-four correspondents.

10. With thanks to Columbia student Eri Kaneko, November 26, 2002, and John Lloyd, "France's Risky War of Independence," *Financial Times*, February 12–13, 2005. See table 1, page 42.

11. However, editors with imagination can reach beyond the standard wire service fare. Assessing the Australian press, Misha Schubert found "there was a surprisingly large amount of copy reprinted from other major international news outlets—Agence France-Presse, *Washington Post*, *New York Times*, *Times* of London, the *Telegraph*, and the *Guardian.*"

12. One 1982 study of U.S. news in the media of nine countries showed that the Indian press was the most interested in home angle stories and that German Democratic Republic (East Germany) newspapers were the least interested. The countries in order of "home angle" stories from the United States in our survey were India, Canada, USSR, Great Britain, Switzerland, German Federal Republic, Australia, France, and German Democratic Republic. See Stephen Hess, "How Foreign Correspondents Cover the United States," *Transatlantic Perspectives*, December 1983, pp. 3–5, reprinted in Hess, *News and Newsmaking* (Brookings, 1996).

13. Editorial, *Philippine Daily Inquirer*, October 23, 2001.

14. "Why Do People Hate America?" *Philippine Star*, November 7, 2002.

15. "Why Is America Hated?" *Hindustan Times*, November 12, 2001.

16. "The Unloved America," *Le Monde*, November 24, 2001.

17. James W. Ceaser, "A Genealogy of Anti-Americanism," *Public Interest* (Summer 2003): 6, quotes Hamilton: "Men admired as profound philosophers gravely asserted that all animals, and with them the human species, degenerate in America."

18. Simon Schama, "The Unloved American," *New Yorker*, March 10, 2003, p. 34.

19. October 17, 2002.

20. Martin Burcharth, "Between Hammer and Anvil," *Correspondence: An International Review of Culture and Society* [Council on Foreign Relations] (Winter 2002–03): 16.

21. *Semana* (Bogota), September 14, 2001, translated and reprinted in *World Press Review* (November 2001), p. 41. In Argentina, the editor of *3 Puntos*, Daniel Gonzalez, wrote that "many intellectuals, journalists, and members of the upper middle-class Argentines" look upon 9/11 as "they deserve it."

22. T. R. Reid, "A Curious Coupling: Brits Take to American Art," *Washington Post*, March 17, 2002. Also see "Why They Hate Us: A Special Report," *National Journal*, September 29, 2001, and Fouad Ajami, "The Falseness of Anti-Americanism," *Foreign Policy* (September–October 2003): 52–61.

23. November 12, 2001.

24. See Stephen Hess and Marvin Kalb, editors, *The Media and the War on Terrorism* (Brookings, 2003), pp. 200, 202.

25. Lecture at the Brookings Institution, May 8, 2002.

26. L. Edwin Atwood, "News of U.S. and Japan in Each Other's Papers," *Gazette* 39 (1987): 73–89; Vernone M. Sparkes, "The Flow of News between Canada and the United States," *Journalism Quarterly* 55 (Summer 1978): 260–68; James W. Markham, "Foreign News in the United Sates and South American Press," *Public Opinion Quarterly* 25 (Summer 1961): 249–62. Also see Jim A. Hart, "Foreign News in U.S. and English Daily Newspapers," *Journalism Quarterly* 43 (1966): 443–48; Ronald G. Hicks and Avishag Gordon, "Foreign News Content in Israeli and U.S. Newspapers," *Journalism Quarterly* 51 (1974): 639–44; George Gerbner and George Marvanyi, "The Many Worlds of the World's Press," *Journal of Communication* 27 (Winter 1977): 52–66.

THEN

1. Donald A. Lambert, "Foreign Correspondents Covering the United States," *Journalism Quarterly* 33 (Summer 1956): 349–56. Unpublished work on foreign correspondents in the United States includes Chung W. Suh, "The Socio-Professional Aspects of Foreign Correspondents in the U.S.: A Study of International Communication," Ph.D. dissertation, University of Minnesota, 1970; Shailendra Ghorpade, "Reporting America for the World: A Survey of Washington-Based Foreign Correspondents," M.A. thesis, University of North Carolina at Chapel Hill, 1983; Neil Griffith Conway, "Foreign Correspondents' Opinion of Foreign News in the U.S. Media," M.A. thesis, University of Maryland, 1983; Wenbing Chen, "A Socio-Professional Portrait of the Washington, D.C., Foreign Correspondent," Ph.D. dissertation, University of Missouri–Columbia, 1995.

2. Hamid Mowlana, "Who Covers America?" *Journal of Communication* 25 (Summer 1975): 86–91.

3. Mary Euyang Shen's survey of 235 correspondents found that the average foreign correspondent's salary was $30,000 a year, which, she concluded, compared with "earnings of American journalists in urban centers in 1977 . . . in the neighborhood of $25,000." Ms. Shen worked at the Foreign Press Center.

4. Lorna Bratvold, "Close-Up of the Washington Reporters," *Carleton Journalism Review* 1 (Summer 1978): 3–9. Another early study interviewed journalists who

reported from the United Nations in New York, but only nine were foreign correspondents, six of whom said that their stories also concentrated on their home country's interests. See Ronald Rubin, "The UN Correspondents," *Western Political Quarterly* 17 (December 1964): 615–31.

5. See "Foreign Correspondents: The News about Us," in Stephen Hess, *News and Newsmaking* (Brookings, 1996), pp. 95–98.

6. Quoted in Carlin Romano, "Assignment: America," *Washington Post,* October 14, 1979.

7. Nine of ten Massachusetts trips were to Boston, all California trips were to Los Angeles or San Francisco, all Michigan trips were to Detroit, all Washington state trips were to Seattle, and three of four Louisiana trips were to New Orleans. That did not change measurably in our follow-up interviews in 1982, although correspondents increased their trips to the West Coast, notably to Los Angeles, reflecting the change in president from Carter to Reagan.

8. Thomas B. Littlewood, "Exploring the Mysterious West, or, How the Foreign Press Corps Sees America," *Saturday Review,* April 15, 1972, p. 26.

9. Shailendra Ghorpade, "Foreign Correspondents Cover Washington for World," *Journalism Quarterly* 61 (Autumn 1984): 667–71, and "Sources and Access: How Foreign Correspondents Rate Washington, D.C.," *Journal of Communication* 34 (Autumn 1984): 32–40. Subsequent published scholarly articles include Murali Nair, "The Foreign Media Correspondent: Dateline Washington D.C.," *Gazette* 48 (1991): 59–64, and Lars Willnat and David Weaver, "Through Their Eyes: The Work of Foreign Correspondents in the United States," *Journalism* 4, no. 4 (2003): 403–22.

10. David Morrison, "Foreign Media Correspondents Based in London," City University, London, unpublished, 1981, p. 24.

11. Patrick Brogan, "Foreign Correspondents in Washington," an occasional paper of the Media Studies Project (Washington: Woodrow Wilson International Center for Scholars, undated but apparently 1989).

12. See Alistair Cooke, *The Americans: Fifty Talks on Our Life and Times* (Knopf, 1979), especially pp. 3–10, and Reuters, "Alistair Cooke Sending 2,000th 'Letter from America,' " *New York Times,* June 19, 1987.

13. See Sam Lipski, "Washington as Seen by Foreigners," *Atlas World Press Review,* August 1974, p. 56. Also see Brandon's fascinating memoir of his years as a foreign correspondent in Washington, *Special Relationships* (New York: Atheneum, 1988).

14. See James Srodes, "The Faker of Fleet Street," *Washington Post,* Outlook section, July 9, 1978.

15. Tom Squitieri, "TASS: Is It a News Agency or Spy Network?" Lowell (Mass.) *Sun,* February 22 and 23, 1982; R. W. Apple Jr., "K.G.B. Spy Defects and British Order 25 Russians Home," *New York Times,* September 13, 1985; and David W. Dunlap, "Soviet Journalists Lament Travel Curbs," *New York Times,* November 21, 1983. Also see John E. Cooney, "A Russian View," *Wall Street Journal,* August 29, 1979, and M. L. Stein, "The Soviet KGB and the Press," *Editor and Publisher,* October 26, 1985, pp. 11, 24.

16. See Tom Dunkel, "The Invisible Press Corps," *Washington Journalism Review,* November 1980, p. 48.

17. Bob Warner, "The Foreign Press in the U.S.A.," *Editor and Publisher,* May 21, 1960, p. 66. This was a four-part series, with other articles appearing on May 28, June 4, and June 11.

18. Wilson Velloso, "Interpreter Translates Appeal into Action," *Washington Post,* September 27, 1981.

19. Quoted in Dom Bonafede, "Foreign Correspondents in Washington Tell the World about the United States," *National Journal,* February 23, 1985, p. 421.

20. Quoted in Romano, "Assignment: America."

21. Barbara Gamarekian, "Working Profile: Marino de Medici," *New York Times,* August 10, 1986.

22. John Cole, "The BBC's War over Words," *Washington Post,* May 19, 1982.

23. Quoted in David Walsh, "Strangers in a Strange Town," *Topic* (World Press Institute, Macalester College, St. Paul, Minnesota: December 1982), p. 4.

24. Littlewood, "Exploring the Mysterious West," p. 25.

25. Jean-Francois Lisee, "The Parochial American: For Foreign Reporters, Covering the U.S. Means Being Ignored," *Washington Post,* Outlook section, November 13, 1988.

26. Quoted in Littlewood, "Exploring the Mysterious West," pp. 24–25.

27. Quoted in Jane Mayer, "Election Baffles Foreign Reporters," *Wall Street Journal,* June 18, 1984. Also see "Translating the Electoral Process," *New York Times,* May 22, 1984.

PATTERNS

1. *Editor and Publisher International Year Book* data should be used only to trace trends. Fluctuations in the number of correspondents from year to year suggest imperfections in compiling the data, especially for Japanese correspondents. Also, the *Year Book* continued to list correspondents under "Soviet Union" until 1995.

2. See Stephen Hess, *International News and Foreign Correspondents* (Brookings, 1996), especially chapter 3.

3. Fifty-five percent of the foreign correspondents listed in *Editor and Publisher International Year Book* in 1998 lived in New York, 45 percent in Washington.

4. See figure 3, "Characteristics of Full-Time Correspondents, 1999," page 33, and figure 1, "Characteristics of Part-Time Correspondents, 1999," page 44.

5. The *Congressional Directory* in 2003–04 listed seventy journalists for U.K. television, forty-five for Japan, and forty-three for Germany. Their biggest bureaus were BBC (thirty-six), Reuters TV (twenty-six), German Television/ARD (sixteen), German Television/ZDF (fifteen), and NHK-Japan Broadcasting (thirteen).

6. Interview, June 18, 2002.

7. The top five newspapers read on a daily basis by full-time foreign correspondents were, in rounded percentages: *New York Times* (seventy-eight), *Washington Post* (forty), *Wall Street Journal* (twenty-nine), *Los Angeles Times* (twenty-one), *Financial Times* (fourteen). The top five magazines were *Time* (sixty-four), *Newsweek* (sixty-three), *Economist* (twenty-four), *U.S. News and World Report* (twenty-four), *New Yorker* (twenty-four). National Public Radio was listened to by fifty-two percent of the respondents.

8. Interview, August 2, 2002.

9. Interview, July 12, 2003. Patrick Smyth, *Irish Times,* made a similar point about the study of journalism in Ireland (interview, July 22, 2002). However, French and Swedish journalists of the same generation reported that they had journalism degrees from schools in their countries.

10. Interview, July 29, 2002.

11. Interview, August 13, 2002.

12. Interview, August 14, 2002.

13. Interview, August 10, 2002.

14. Interview, June 5, 2002.

15. Interview, June 4, 2002.

16. Interview, June 21, 2002.

17. Interview, June 14, 2002.

18. Stanley Washburn, *The Cable Game* (Boston: Sherman French, 1912), p. 14.

19. Ryszard Kapuscinski, *The Soccer War* (Knopf, 1991), p. 130.

20. Interview, February 23, 1998.

21. Clyde H. Farnsworth, "How the Japanese Gain Perspective on Covering America," *New York Times*, May 27, 1987.

22. See Frank J. Prial, "Alistair Cooke, Elegant Interpreter of America, Dies at 95," *New York Times*, March 31, 2004.

23. Interview with Shigeru Komago, bureau chief, February 19, 1998.

24. Stephen Hess and Marvin Kalb, editors, *The Media and the War on Terrorism* (Brookings, 2003), p. 212.

25. Interview, October 8, 2002.

26. Interviews, April 6, 1999, and e-mail April 22, 2004.

27. Quoted in Anne E. Rumsey, "In Person, Wolf Blitzer," *National Journal*, April 25, 1987, p. 1013.

28. Interview, July 25, 2002. Hillel Kuttler also was Washington correspondent for the *Jerusalem Post* for six years beginning in 1993; he is now a freelance writer in Baltimore (survey response, May 4, 1999, and e-mail April 22, 2004). Jonathan Broder, Washington correspondent for *Jerusalem Report* in 1999, subsequently went to work for MSNBC and *Congressional Quarterly*.

29. Interview, October 10, 2002.

30. Interview, July 22, 2002.

31. Interview, November 1, 2002.

32. Interview, February 26, 1998.

33. Interview, May 2, 2002.

34. Interview, July 29, 2002.

35. Dergham made these comments on "Caught in the Crossfire," a PBS documentary about Arab Americans after the 9/11 attacks. See www.pbs.org/itvs/caughtinthecrossfire/raghida.html [September 2, 2005]. Among others who commented on the expatriate experience was Jorge Banales, who was born in Montevideo, Uruguay, and had lived in Washington since 1981: "If I had stayed in our country, I don't know if I would be alive" (interview, June 4, 2002).

IRREGULARS

1. Survey response with documentation, May 6, 1999. He was a Washington correspondent, ANSA, Italian News Agency, 1960–64, and U.S. correspondent, *Il Tempo* (Rome), 1964–87.

2. Survey response with documentation, May 17, 1999.

3. Survey response with documentation, May 1, 1999.

4. Survey response, June 4, 1999.

5. Survey response with documentation, June 19, 1999.

6. Interview, July 10, 2002.

7. Survey response, May 8, 1999, with documentation.

8. Survey response, June 20, 1999.

9. Survey response, May 18, 1999, with documentation.

10. Survey response, May 12, 1999, with documentation.

11. Interview, August 10, 2002.

12. Interview, December 4, 2001, and survey response, March 23, 1999.

13. Survey response, June 14, 1999, with documentation.

14. Survey response, May 4, 1999, with documentation. An article about an exhibition that Solomon curated vividly described some of her resume: "She was speaking in her Upper East Side apartment, surrounded by an eclectic art collection and boxes full of the seven books she has written. They include *The Beat of Life*, a 1960 novel about an unplanned pregnancy, and *Arriving Where We Started*, a 1972 memoir about her involvement in the resistance to Franco's rule when she lived in Europe for several years

after World War II. Among other adventures, Ms. Solomon worked on the underground magazine *Peninsula*, published in Paris by exiled Spanish dissidents." Felicia R. Lee, "Women of Little Magazines and Big Ideas," *New York Times*, October 9, 2004.

15. Margaret Engel, "America's Babel of Ethnic Voices," *World & I*, August 1, 2003, p. 62.

16. See Ron Feemster, "Found in Translation" and "A Guide to Ethnic Media," *Ford Foundation Report*, Spring 2004, pp. 4–5.

17. Survey responses: April 8, 1999, March 30, 1999, August 11, 1999.

18. Survey response with documentation, undated, but the article appeared April 30, 2003.

19. Survey response, May 7, 1999.

20. Survey response, June 28, 1999.

21. Seife responded to our survey May 4, 1999. He later moved to an American magazine, *Science*, and wrote a critically acclaimed book, *Zero: The Biography of a Dangerous Idea* (Viking, 2000).

22. Survey response, August 3, 1999.

23. Survey response, June 16, 1999.

24. Survey response, July 2, 1999, with documentation.

25. Unsigned, "Yve Janssens Laudy," *Washington Post*, September 3, 2004.

26. Stephen Hess, *International News and Foreign Correspondents* (Brookings, 1996) offers a typology of the freelance writer for an American news organization: the spouse, the expert, the adventurer, the flinger ("a person off on a fling"), the ideologue, and the resident (pp. 68–70). It includes a list of distinguished foreign correspondents, including Daniel Schorr and Stanley Karnow, who started as freelancers (p. 74).

27. Charlie Torrini, survey response, June 4, 1999.

28. Tony Perrottet, survey response, June 15, 1999.

29. Our 1999 survey showed that 64 percent of full-time foreign correspondents discussed their most recent story with the home office before publication, but only 47 percent of the part-timers (irregulars) did.

HOLLYWOOD

1. Edmund L. Andrews, "Hollywood Tales Just Fiction, German Paper Says," *New York Times*, June 2, 2000.

2. Louis B. Hobson, "60th Annual Golden Globes: The Golden Years," *Calgary Sun*, March 17, 2004.

3. Press release, undated, Michael Russell Group, 292 South La Cienega Blvd., Beverly Hills, California 90211.

4. Members must reside in Southern California, be a Hollywood correspondent of a publication published outside the United States, and produce at least four articles a year for which they are paid.

5. Dana Harris, "Helmut Voss," *The Hollywood Reporter Golden Globes Special Issue*, January 19–25, 1999.

6. Sharon Waxman, "Golden Globes Group Seeks More Respect—and Money," *Washington Post*, December 19, 2002.

7. Sharon Waxman, "Lobbying for Golden Globes Is a Hollywood Ritual," *New York Times*, January 13, 2004.

8. Debra Kaufman, "From the Source," *The Hollywood Reporter Golden Globes Special Issue*, January 19–25, 1999.

9. Emily Farache, "Golden Globes on Sharon Stone Watch," *Eonline*, December 21, 1999.

10. Waxman, "Lobbying for Golden Globes."

11. Rick Lyman and Laura M. Holson, "Globes Make Worldbeaters of 2 Films," *New York Times,* January 21, 2003.

12. See Ginia Bellafante, "Golden Globes, on a Budget," *New York Times,* January 25, 2004.

13. Waxman, "Golden Globes Group Seeks More Respect."

14. Alessandra Stanley, "Thanks to the Fans, the Family, the Dog, the Goldfish . . . ," *New York Times,* December 13, 2003, and Adam Buckman, "The Best Awards Money Can Buy," *New York Post,* December 9, 2003. The documentary was directed and narrated by Vikram Jayanti and aired on the Trio channel December 2003–January 2004.

15. Quoted in Julie Scelfo, "Golden Global Politics," *Brill's Content,* February 2001, p. 46.

16. Peter Bart, "The Global Gatekeepers," *Variety,* December 22, 2003–January 2, 2004.

17. "Saverio Lomedico," *Variety,* June 22, 1999. The movies listed by tvguide.com are *September Affair* (1950) and *A Patch of Blue* (1965).

18. See Wesley Morris, "In Search of Dirty Secrets, 'Globes' Fails to Strike Gold," *Boston Globe,* December 13, 2003.

19. Richard Horgan, "Golden Shutterbug" (www.filmstew.com [September 10, 2003]).

IN AMERICA

1. Interview, July 22, 2002.

2. Interview, July 19, 2002. Steyn was Washington correspondent for National Media of South Africa.

3. However, the question does not sort out whether they studied in the United States before or after they became foreign correspondents.

4. Interview, July 19, 2002.

5. Interview, August 6, 2002.

6. Interview, July 12, 2003.

7. Survey response, July 2, 1999.

8. Survey response, May 10, 1999.

9. Survey response, May 1, 1999.

10. Survey response, June 17, 1999.

11. See Stephen Hess, *International News and Foreign Correspondents* (Brookings, 1996), p. 14.

12. Interview, August 14, 2002.

13. Survey response, June 17, 1999.

14. National stereotypes, of course, are an American habit as well. The foreign correspondents were also asked to describe the stereotypes of their own countries that they saw in the U.S. media. Among the responses: "friendly, lazy, macho beer drinkers" (Australia); "Nazi-country where everybody is singing and skiing" (Austria); "pretentious, self-centered, think their culture still dominates the world" (France); "rigid, chauvinistic, dull" (Japan); and "Dracula country" (Romania).

15. Interview, August 8, 2002.

16. Interview, August 7, 2002.

17. Interview, August 13, 2002.

18. Interview, August 14, 2002.

19. Interview, October 16, 2002.

20. Survey response, October 20, 1999.

21. Interview, July 3, 2002.

22. Philip Seib, *Beyond the Front Lines: How the News Media Cover a World Shaped by War* (Palgrave Macmillan, 2004), p. 20.

23. Interview, June 14, 2002.

24. Interview, June 14, 2002.

25. Interview, July 19, 2002.

26. Interview, July 1, 2002.

27. Interview, June 10, 2002. At that time, his wife had just received a master's degree in public health from Johns Hopkins University and was hoping to find a job with "companies who are developing health programs for third world countries."

28. Interview, July 11, 2002.

29. Interview, August 8, 2002.

30. Hess, *International News and Foreign Correspondents*, pp. 24–25.

31. The survey results (372 responses) were 0–7 days (15.3 percent), 8–31 days (48.1 percent), 32–60 days (22.0 percent), and 61+ days (14.5 percent). The results for full-time and part-time correspondents were quite similar.

32. Interview, July 16, 2002.

33. Interview, June 13, 2002.

34. Interview, June 18, 2002.

35. Interview, July 11, 2002.

36. Interview, August 10, 2002.

37. Interview, June 4, 2002.

38. Interview, August 2, 2002.

39. Interview, August 24, 2002.

40. Interview, August 13, 2002.

41. Interview, June 26, 2002.

42. Interview, August 10, 2002.

43. Michel Faure, "The Leftist and the Gipper," *France* (Fall 2004): p. 11 (publication of the French embassy, Washington).

44. Survey response, May 2, 1999.

TIME

1. Interview, August 7, 2002.

2. Interview, July 29, 2002.

3. Interview, June 5, 2002.

4. Interview, June 14, 2002.

5. Interview, July 24, 2002.

6. Interview, August 10, 2002.

7. Interview, August 14, 2002.

CONTACT

1. Interview, August 14, 2002.

2. There is a more common use of the term "the CNN effect" in research on political communication and in international relations referring to whether continuous news saturation influences government actions, particularly in humanitarian situations. See Steven Livingston, "Clarifying the CNN Effect: An Examination of Media Effects According to Type of Military Intervention," Research Paper R-18, Shorenstein Center on Press, Politics, and Public Policy, Harvard University, June, 1997, and Piers Robinson, *The CNN Effect: The Myth of News, Foreign Policy, and Intervention* (Routledge, 2002).

3. Interview, July 19, 2002.

174   NOTES

4. Interview, July 21, 2002.
5. Interview, July 11, 2002.
6. Interview, July 12, 2003.
7. Interview, August 2, 2002.
8. Interview, July 13, 2002.
9. Interview, July 4, 2002.
10. Interview, August 14, 2002.
11. Interview, July 14, 2002.
12. Survey response, May 2, 1999.
13. Interview, July 26, 2002.
14. Interview, August 10, 2002.
15. Interview, July 1, 2002.
16. Interview, July 19, 2002.
17. Albert L. May, *The Virtual Trail: Political Journalism on the Internet* (Institute for Politics, Democracy, and the Internet, George Washington University, 2002), p. 9.
18. Interview, August 8, 2002.
19. Letter to author, July 1, 1999.

ACCESS

1. See Stephen Hess, *The Washington Reporters* (Brookings, 1981), p. 2.
2. Interview, July 3, 2002.
3. Interview, July 18, 2002.
4. Interview, July 29, 2002. Independently, Yan Feng of China's Xinhua News Agency made the same point about press relations in India (interview, August 13, 2002).
5. Interview, July 19, 2002.
6. Interview, February 26, 1998.
7. Interview, November 18, 2003. Translated from the Russian by Anna Loukianova, a Brookings Institution intern.
8. Interview, October 1, 2002. Also see Jane Perlez and Jim Rutenberg, "U.S. Courts Network It Once Described as 'All Osama,' " *New York Times,* March 20, 2003.
9. Secretary of State Colin Powell also gave Al Arabiya an exclusive interview on May 13, 2004, which was conducted by Hisham Melhem, the Washington bureau chief of *An-Nahar* (a daily newspaper in Lebanon), who hosts a weekly "talk show from Washington" for the network. Also see Samantha M. Shapiro, "The War inside the Arab Newsroom," *New York Times Magazine,* January 2, 2005.
10. Interview, July 1, 2002.
11. Interview, June 26, 2002.
12. Interview, July 11, 2002.
13. The journalists were from the *Globe and Mail* (Canada), *Al-Ahram* (Egypt), *The Straits Times* (Singapore), *Svenska Dagbladet* (Sweden), and *Hurriyet* (Turkey).
14. Interview, July 22, 2003.
15. Interview, July 22, 2002.
16. Interview, July 19, 2002.
17. Interview, June 14, 2002.
18. *Washington Post,* November 15, 2003.
19. Interview, April 28, 1980.
20. Interview, July 22, 2002.
21. Interview, March 22, 1999.
22. Catherine Eisele, "For Foreign Reporters, Washington Is Surprisingly Open—and Confusing," *The Hill,* April 16, 1997, pp. 20–21.

23. Survey response, May 8, 1999.

24. Anne E. Rumsey, "Journalistic Go-Between Straddles Two Cultures," *National Journal*, April 25, 1987, p. 1013. Also see Wolf Blitzer, "The Journalist and the Spy," *Washington Journalism Review*, May 1989, pp. 29–34. The *Jerusalem Post*'s Janine Zacharia on niche access: "So when [policymakers] want to talk to Israelis or Jewish Americans or Jews in general, they see the advantage in talking to us" (interview, July 25, 2002).

25. Interview with Betty Brannan Jaen, July 22, 2002.

26. Interview, August 8, 2002.

27. Interview, July 19, 2002.

28. Interview, June 26, 2002.

29. Interview, June 26, 2002.

30. Interview, June 13, 2002.

31. Interview, August 8, 2002.

32. Interview, July 22, 2003.

33. Interview, August 14, 2002.

34. Interview, June 10, 2002.

35. Interview, October 8, 2002.

36. Dana Milbank, "Wrapping Up Tough Questions with Foil," *Washington Post*, January 22, 2002. Among the other foreign correspondent "foils" listed by Milbank were Connie Lawn, an American who says she reports for outlets including *Cape Talk* (South Africa) and Radio Pacific (New Zealand), and Jacobo Goldstein of Honduras. "I didn't take it personally, my fifteen minutes of fame," Goldstein told us. "Every press secretary that I've covered, and I've covered them all since Larry Speakes [under Reagan], when they get accosted they jump and try to [maneuver]. . . . But it didn't bother me. You'd be surprised how many people came to [defend me]. I didn't realize I had so many friends" (interview, August 6, 2002).

37. Carl P. Leubsdorf, "Political Posing Turns White House Press Briefings into 'Absurd Plays,' " *Baltimore Sun*, July 31, 1978.

38. Interview, October 24, 2002.

39. Interview, June 4, 2002.

40. Interview, May 1999.

41. Interview, March 18, 1999.

42. Interview, July 11, 2002.

43. Christina Ianzito, "Strangers in a Strange Land," *Capital Style*, April 1999, pp. 19–20.

44. Interview, March 17, 1999.

45. Interview, March 29, 1998.

46. Interview, July 3, 2002.

HELP

1. E-mail response, May 20, 1999.

2. Interview, February 4, 2002.

3. Letter, May 27, 1999.

4. E-mail response, May 18, 1999.

5. Zeynep Alemdar, "Conveniences for Correspondents," *Washington Post*, September 23, 1986.

6. E-mail response, October 8, 1999.

7. E-mail response, June 22, 1999.

8. E-mail response, May 22, 1999.

9. E-mail response, May 22, 1999.

10. Interview, February 21, 2002.

11. E-mail response from Irawan Nugroho, *Gamma Weekly News Magazine,* May 19, 1999.

12. E-mail response from Charles Groenhuijsen, NOS Dutch Public Broadcasting, May 21, 1999.

13. E-mail response from Paolo Mastrolilli, Vatican Radio, May 18, 1999.

14. E-mail response from Ian Brodie, *London Times,* May 22, 1999.

15. E-mail response from Andrew Viscount, L'Espresso Publishing Group, Italy, May 24, 1999.

16. Interview, January 17, 2002.

17. The budget for the FPC in FY2001, excluding staff salaries, was $594,760.

18. Dhiman Chattopadhyay, "City Takes Crash Course from Cleveland," *Times of India,* March 14, 2002. Also see Jaideep Mazumdar, "Can Kolkata Do a Cleveland Spin?" *Hindustan Times,* March 15, 2002.

19. E-mail response, May 24, 1999.

20. Here is a sample of IJNet listings: "The AAAS Science Radio Journalism Fellowship is underwritten by the South African government, and enables local journalists to travel to Washington, D.C., to specialize in science reporting" . . . "The Douglas Tweedale Memorial Fellowship was created to enhance the professional development of promising Latin American journalists" . . . "Three-week program, held each year in June, for journalists of Japan's English-language press." We counted sixty-five programs, including invitations to study at such elite institutions as Duke, Emory, Harvard, the University of Michigan, and Stanford.

BORROWED NEWS AND THE INTERNET

1. Survey response, May 4, 1999.

2. A 1988 American Press Institute survey of 115 foreign correspondents in the United States found daily newspapers and weekly news magazines "prime sources of information." See Mike Hughes, "Most Foreign Correspondents in U.S. Like the Papers They Read Here," *presstime,* December 1989, p. 47.

3. Ambrose Evans-Prichard, " 'What Does *The Post* Say?' How Foreign Correspondents Report Washington," *National Interest* (Spring 1988): 117.

4. See Robert M. Entman, *Projections of Power* (University of Chicago, 2004), p. 18.

5. Survey response, May 4, 1999.

6. Survey response, May 7, 1999.

7. Survey response, May 4, 1999.

8. Survey response, May 28, 1999.

9. Survey response, May 4, 1999.

10. Survey response, May 1, 1999.

11. Survey response, May 7, 1999.

12. E-mail response from Rui Coimbra, July 8, 1999.

13. See Albert L. May, *The Virtual Trail: Political Journalism on the Internet* (Institute for Politics, Democracy, and the Internet, George Washington University, 2002).

14. Survey response from Pamela Glass, May 17, 1999.

15. Survey response from Jose M. Passos, June 17, 1999.

ONE DAY

1. The respondents' stories were for Algeria, Argentina, Australia, Austria, Belgium, Brazil, Bulgaria, Canada, Chile, China, Colombia, Croatia, Czech Republic, Denmark, Egypt, Finland, France, Germany, Greece, Guatemala, Hong Kong (listed separately

from China), Hungary, India, Indonesia, Ireland, Israel, Italy, Japan, Kuwait, Lebanon, Lithuania, Macedonia, Mali, Mauritania, Mexico, Netherlands, New Zealand, Nigeria, Norway, Pakistan, Philippines, Poland, Portugal, Romania, Russia, Saudi Arabia, Senegal, Serbia, Slovakia, South Africa, South Korea, Spain, Sweden, Switzerland, Taiwan, Thailand, Turkey, United Arab Emirates, United Kingdom, Vatican City, and Venezuela.

2. Translated from the French: "Ereinté par la critique, assailli par les fans, le film arrive dans une Amérique hystérique."

3. Letter, June 29, 1999.

4. Peter Schibli, survey response, May 6, 1999.

5. Hugues-Denver Akassy, survey response, May 5, 1999.

6. Shin Hara, survey response, June 18, 1999.

7. Translation provided by ORT/Russian Public TV, June 10, 1999.

8. Gintautas Alksninis, survey response, June 18, 1999.

9. Jerome Hule, survey response, June 4, 1999.

10. Luis M. Pires, survey response, May 23, 1999.

11. Lucas Mendes, survey response, May 4, 1999.

12. Tomi Ervamaa, survey response, May 19, 1999.

13. Charles Wheelan, survey response, May 14, 1999. See "Free Speech: Can Media Kill?" *Economist*, May 15, 1999, pp. 26–27.

14. Survey response, May 15, 1999.

15. Alberto Garcia Marrder, survey response, May 23, 1999.

16. Ian Brodie, "30-Hour Mission—Then Home in Time for Tea," *London Times*, May 10, 1999.

17. Michael Rice, *Reporting U.S.-European Relations: Four Nations, Four Newspapers* (Pergamon Press, 1982), p. xxxi.

18. Alf B. Johnsen, survey response, July 15, 1999.

19. Nicole O'Neill, survey response, August 3, 1999.

20. Cesar Romero, survey response, October 18, 1999.

21. Draft report, "Symposium on Leadership in Mexico-U.S. Journalism," Washington, Woodrow Wilson International Center for Scholars, October 29, 2003.

22. Jan Cienski, "Buchanan Enters Crowded Republican Presidential Race," *National Post*, March 3, 1999.

23. Barbara G. B. Ferguson, survey response, June 22, 1999.

N O W

1. Chung Woo Suh, "The Socio-Professional Aspects of Foreign Correspondents in the U.S.," Ph.D. dissertation, University of Minnesota, 1970.

2. Paddy Smith, "Feeding in the Peripatetic Press Tent: On Being an Irish Foreign Correspondent," *Studies: An Irish Quarterly Review* (Spring 2004): 90.

3. Karin L. Johnston, "Clashing Worlds and Images: Media and Politics in the United States and Germany," *Issue Brief*, August 2004, p. 5 (American Institute for Contemporary German Studies, Johns Hopkins University). Also see John Lloyd, "Europe's Intellects Unite!" *Financial Times*, January 31, 2003.

4. See, for example, "Reuters' India Expansion Involves U.S. Layoffs," *presstime*, October 2004, p. 20: "Reuters Group PLC announced plans to add 40 to 60 staff positions to its facility in Bangalore, India, to increase its U.S. equities coverage of small and mid-cap companies. The financial news service will eliminate as many as 20 positions from its U.S. and European offices."

5. Doug Saunders, "Media Descend on California Recall Vote," *Globe and Mail*, October 7, 2003.

6. Jeff Kearns, "Pressing Questions," *Sacramento News and Review*, August 14, 2003.

7. Cathy Trost and Alicia C. Shepard, *Running toward Danger: Stories behind the Breaking News of 9/11* (Rowman and Littlefield, 2002), pp. 212 and 216.

8. Michiko Kakutani, "Now Americans May Read What Alistair Cooke Told the British about Them," *New York Times*, November 7, 1979.

9. Hiroshi Fujita, "Press Responsibility for the Perception Gap," *Japan Review of International Affairs* 9 (Winter 1995): 48.

10. For example, Washington correspondent Vittorio Zucconi of the influential, left-leaning Italian daily *La Repubblica* (January 12, 2002): "Bush has begun fighting to defend himself from the growing suspicion that the most serious company failure in U.S. history [Enron] may be a history of political corruption that goes right to the heart of the Bush Team, through the formidable gas pipelines of electoral funds."

11. Blake Morrison, "This Time, There Were Cameras . . . ," *Guardian*, September 14, 2001.

12. Rime Allaf, "Dangerous Delusions," *Daily Star*, October 3, 2001, reprinted in *World Press Review*, October 3, 2001.

13. "No Challenges to the United States," *Mail and Guardian*, September 14, 2001, reprinted in *World Press Review*, November 2001, p. 14.

Thanks

First, my thanks to those who have made Brookings such a glorious place to think and work. In the Governance Studies Program: Gladys Arrisueno, Sarah Binder, E. J. Dionne, Bethany Hase, Robert Katzmann, Paul Light, Thomas Mann, Pietro Nivola, and Kent Weaver. At the Brookings Press, my editor, Eileen Hughes, and her colleagues Larry Converse, Robert Faherty, Christopher Kelaher, Janet Walker, and Susan Woollen. Special people in the Brookings Library include Sarah Chilton, Eric Eisinger, and Mary Fry. Research assistants during different phases of the study were Bonnie Eley, Elizabeth Galewski, and Daniel Reilly.

My youngest colleagues, the interns (some of whom have had notable careers since their days with me) were Peter Beinart (Yale), Michael Falcone (UCLA), Erica Gaston (Stanford), Charles Hess (Columbia), Seth Laughlin (University of North Carolina), Anna Loukianova (Thiel College), Afshin Mohamadi (University of Michigan), Peter Pozefsky (Harvard), Michael Schwaiger (Cornell), Matthew Segal (Brandeis), Susanna Sigg (Georgetown), Gene Sperling (University of Minnesota), and Dorothee Weiler.

The kind folks who volunteered as translators were David Bair, Josef Braml, Michael Calingaert, Ivo Daalder, Niclas Ericsson, Candice Geouge, Lincoln Gordon, Carol Graham, Susan Jackson, Daniel Jianu, Sun Kordel, Stefano Pettinato, and Tibor Purger.

Among the men and women of the Foreign Press Centers who answered our questions, provided material, and allowed us to look over their shoulders are Frank Baba, Jefferson Brown, Liza Davis, James Ellickson-Brown, Marti Estell, Frank Gomez, Judith Jamison,

179

Haider Karzai, Peter Kovach, Millie McCoo, Douglas McCurrach, M. Chris Mason, Robert Meyers, David E. Miller, George Newman, Kimberly Nisbet, Majorie Ransom, Miriam Rider, Yolanda Robinson, Mary Euyang Shen, JoDell Shields, Katherine Turpin, and Angela Yasuda.

Our questions about the International Press Centers were answered by Sam Kaplan (Seattle), David McCollum (Houston), Patricia Sullivan (Chicago), and Terry Uhl (Cleveland).

The State Department provided the excellent "foreign media reaction" reports, under the direction of Kathleen J. Brahney and Stephen M. Shaffer.

The chapter "Context" could not have been written without Anne Nelson and her students at the Graduate School of Journalism at Columbia University: Francisco Aravena (Chile), Alberto Armendariz (Argentina), Marina Artusa (Argentina), Muhammad Athar Lila (Canada), Kodi Barth (Kenya), Simon Bishop (United Kingdom), Andrew Blackman (United Kingdom), Julian Brookes (United Kingdom), James Brown (United Kingdom), Caroline Chaumont (France), Fang Cui (China), Noemi Cuni (Spain), Mukul Devichand (United Kingdom), Jose Diaz-Briseno (Mexico), Magdalena Eriksson (Sweden), Mariam Fam (Egypt), Caryn Farber (Israel), Marta Ferrer (Panama), Sarah Gilbert (Australia), Diego Graglia (Argentina), Seema Gupta (Singapore), Soyoung Ho (South Korea), Fahd Husain (Pakistan), M. Kalyanaraman (India), Eri Kaneko (Japan), Piya Kochlar (India), Svetlana Kolchik (Russia), Aude Lagorce (France), Leila Lak (United Kingdom), Alejandro Loinaz (Philippines), Belen Lopez Garrido (Spain), Kayo Matsushita (Japan), Maureen Mitra (India), Muneeza Naqvi (India), Jasima Nielsen (Denmark), Pema Norbu (Bhutan), Jenny Nordberg (Sweden), Kayode Ogunbunmi (Nigeria), Mary Christine O. Ong (Philippines), Noel T. Pangilinan (Philippines), Ferreira Patino (Brazil), Jeannette Platou (Norway), Lauren Quaintance (New Zealand), Maria Ramirez (Italy), Carla Ranicki (United Kingdom), Claudio Remeseira (Argentina) Gabriel Rodriguez-Nava (Mexico), Luis Sarmiento (Colombia), Misha Schubert (Australia), Alexandra Simo-Barry (United Kingdom), Yasser Sobhi (Egypt), Tessa van Staden (South Africa), Kosuke Takahashi (Japan), Hide Tamura (Japan), Clara Tarrero (Spain), Ke Xu (China), Li Yuan (China), Katerina Zachovalova (Czech Republic), Mariana van Zeller (Portugal).

Among the diplomats in Washington who explained their countries' media and provided us with material were Jose Abro (Philippines), Salvador Adriano (Mozambique), Eltayeb Ahmed (Sudan), Raquel Alfaro (Panama), Nair Al-Jubeir (Saudi Arabia), Dorothy Amini (Malawi), Chary Annaberdiev (Turkmenistan), Patrick Ayendi (Nigeria), Mohammad Azam (Pakistan), James Badou (Côte d'Ivoire), Michel Bagratuni (Armenia), Frederick Bangoura (Guinea), Mukti Bhatta (Nepal), Ricardo Caballero (Paraguay), Fidel Cano (Colombia), James Caulker (Sierra Leone), Jacob Chumba (Kenya), Adolfo Dante Loss (Argentina), John Thomas Dipowe (Botswana), Abel Aleem El Abyad (Egypt), Fernando Flores (Ecuador), Carol Francis (Trinidad and Tobago), Armando Francisco (Angola), Ndinga Gaba (Central African Republic), Faysal Gouia (Tunisia), Kamel Hadri (Algeria), O'Neil D. Hamilton (Jamaica), Limor Hasson (Israel), Malamin K. Juwara (Gambia), Kingsley Karimu (Ghana), H. B. Kim (South Korea), Lorempo Landjerque (Togo), Lauri Lepik (Estonia), Sandi Logan (Australia), Yusup Magdiev (Uzbekistan), Odette Magnet (Chile), Faiza Mehdi (Morocco), Simona-Mirela Miculescu (Romania), Herando Mosca (Brazil), John Mulutula (Zambia), Aya Nakamura (Japan), Daniel Ngwepe (South Africa), Mirtha Virginia Perea (Costa Rica), Mai Sayovongs (Laos), Ausra Semaskiene (Lithuania), Ibrahima Sene (Senegal), Leanid L. Sennikau (Belarus), Mikail Shurgalin (Russia), Petr Silantiev (Russia), Amar Sinha (India), Mahendra Siregar (Indonesia), Kasama Suebwises (Thailand), Crecy Tawah (Cameroon), Thaung Tun (Myanmar), Ricardo Viteri (Guatemala), and Victoria Wicks-Brown (New Zealand).

Others who have been important to us, but in their own categories, are Everette E. Dennis (Fordham), Carl Sessions Stepp (Philip Merrill College of Journalism, University of Maryland), Marvin Kalb (Shorenstein Center, Harvard), David Morrison (City University, London), Marianne Ginsburg (German Marshall Fund), Albert May and Steven Livingston (George Washington University), and Suzanne Adams (Foreign Press Association).

Ultimately, of course, my greatest debt of gratitude is to the foreign correspondents—surveyed, observed, interviewed. Whenever I am in another country and turn on the television or pick up a newspaper, I will remember the goodwill of those who shared their experiences with a stranger.

Index